Other People's Gardens

CHRISTOPHER LLOYD

VIKING

By the same author

THE WELL-TEMPERED GARDEN

THE ADVENTUROUS GARDENER

THE WELL-CHOSEN GARDEN

FOLIAGE PLANTS

THE YEAR AT GREAT DIXTER

CLEMATIS

GARDEN FLOWERS FROM SEED *(with Graham Rice)*

VIKING

Published by the Penguin Group
Penguin Books Ltd, 27 Wrights Lane, London w8 5tz, England
Penguin Books USA Inc., 375 Hudson Street, New York, New York 10014, USA
Penguin Books Australia Ltd, Ringwood, Victoria, Australia
Penguin Books Canada Ltd, 10 Alcorn Avenue, Toronto, Ontario, Canada m4v 3b2
Penguin Books (NZ) Ltd, 182–190 Wairau Road, Auckland 10, New Zealand

Penguin Books Ltd, Registered Offices: Harmondsworth, Middlesex, England

First published 1995
1 3 5 7 9 10 8 6 4 2
First edition

Printed in Great Britain by Butler & Tanner Ltd, Frome, Somerset
Set in 10.5/14.25pt Monophoto Bembo by Selwood Systems, Midsomer Norton

A CIP catalogue record for this book is available from the British Library

ISBN 0 670 85618 5

Frontispiece: Chapel Knap. By the conservatory on the top terrace, an urn stands bold
against the blue sea of Porlock Bay. Geraniums, marguerites and verbena tumble over the
terrace wall.

Contents

Photographic Acknowledgements

The author and publishers are grateful to the following for permission to reproduce photographs on the following pages: *Stream Cottage* – David Crampton, 16, 19, 20; *Coldham* – Jack Elliott, 22, 25, 27, 29; *Kingston Maurward* – Fergus Garrett, 72, 73; *Overbecks* – A. Murdoch, 78, 81 (both photographs), 85; *Chapel Knap* – Roy Cheek, 100, 102, 103, 104, Daphne Dunkason, Frontispiece, 105; *Belsay Hall* – Stephen Anderton, 121, 124, 125 bottom photograph, James Mortimer, 126.

All the other photographs in the book were taken by the author.

Preface

MICHAEL WALTER has been my good fairy on several occasions. When Collins were independent publishers, he edited several of my books and coined the title for *The Well-Tempered Garden*. More recently he suggested *Other People's Gardens* both as a good subject for me to tackle and as a good title, which I think it is. It is a good subject because, both in books and in articles, I have written a great deal about my own garden and that can go too far. One needs to look further afield and to assess what other gardeners are doing. Viking/Penguin have, as on many other occasions, backed me up in welcoming a title which they hadn't suggested themselves. Many publishers, these days, seem to have worked out and costed exactly the books they want, even before settling on an author. This makes for uniformity and predictability – advantageous in some ways but with a tendency to iron out individuality.

I have been working on *Other People's Gardens* spasmodically for several years, partly because I don't want to be for ever on the road – indeed, I am by nature stay-at-home, so I have been collecting my notes gradually. In the end, I have covered a fair bit of ground and quite a range of types. I have described only one garden in my own county of Sussex. On the other hand, I have been greatly stimulated by gardens in Australia, New Zealand and America. I visit Scotland on holiday every year, so it wasn't difficult to find worthwhile examples there.

Only a few National Trust or other institutional gardens have been included, and those have been blessed with head gardeners (or whatever grander-sounding title they prefer to adopt) having such strong personalities as to be able to leave their individual stamp on gardens with which they closely identify. For it is the mark of the individual which I find so fascinating. True, there are fashions, which are apt to be followed, but the indvidual's imprint can override much of that. And, where you own your garden, you can please yourself about how you treat it, money and labour (which includes your own) being the only serious constraints.

Most gardeners are warm and generous; certainly all of those I have asked to cooperate for this book. I have immensely enjoyed sharing their gardens with them and all have welcomed my intrusion. Gardeners are great sharers. The researching of *Other People's Gardens* has made me a lot of new friends and I do thank them wholeheartedly for making my task such a pleasure.

You can't write off the top of your head about another garden in the way that you can of your own. Notes have to be read through and assimilated, photographs scrutinized. That gets you back into the feel of the place again so that you are spiritually there, once more, even though your visit(s) was (were) quite a while ago. You don't want to be too out of date, of course, and in a few cases where the owner of a garden I wanted to include has died, I have excluded that garden. John Treasure, a close friend since 1952, is a case in point. As Sir David Scott used to say, 'A garden dies with its owner.' Sad in a way, but I do see a continuing succession of young people ready to take over, metaphorically, where others have left off. Theirs will be the gardening names of the future. The best of them enjoy getting their hands dirty, leading by example, not merely by direction.

We all profit from what we have learned from others but there is always scope for doing things differently ourselves. That is what makes gardening a continuingly creative art.

England: South and East

THE VENTNOR BOTANIC GARDEN

$\longrightarrow\!\!\!>\!\!-\!\!0\!\!-\!\!\ll\!\!\longleftarrow$

O N 15 MAY 1990, ten days after returning from a tour in the south-
west, I ventured across to the Isle of Wight on my own, leaving my
car (which I was assured would be vandalized) in an open park near
the ferry at Portsmouth.

Simon Goodenough met me at Ryde and he and his wife, Deb, gave me
hospitality in their house at Newport that night. They have an infant boy to
whom Deb, with a beatific smile, runs at his smallest squeak. He'll have as
strong a personality as his Pa.

The back of their house is a surprise. From a sitting-out platform it drops
sharply to the River Medina, a few yards below, here a swift-flowing stream
rather than a river, which shortly afterwards expands into a long estuary.

However, from Ryde we drove straight to the south coast at Ventnor (or
St Lawrence, to be accurate), where Simon is curator of the so-called Botanic
Garden. There's nothing botanic about it, but the title must have sounded
pleasantly important to those who decided on it. Simon reckons that the
Island Gardens would be a good title and I agree.

He was a Kew student, renowned for living it up and for a huge capacity
for beer. He was married then but that came unstuck. Deb, his second wife,
is a Canadian from Alberta. What particularly attracted them to Ventnor was
that there were jobs for both of them. Deb does the plant propagation.

I had first met them two years earlier at an International Plant Propagators'
Society conference that we were both attending, and they subsequently visited
me at Dixter. They are good news, and I heard from a gardening friend that
the Ventnor set-up was well worth a visit. *Country Life* said they'd like a piece
on the garden, which I've written but am not referring to as I write this
because I don't like plagiarizing myself. And anyway I can write in a more
personal vein in my own book than I can for a magazine.

The site of the present gardens was a vast Victorian hospital for tubercular
patients started in 1868 and completed around 1900. The men and the women

The Palm Garden with purple
foliage of cannas, acanthus spikes
in flower and soft red watsonias.

were kept strictly separated. The men did a lot of the labouring. An on-site quarry was used to build the terraces and the Wall Garden walls.

After the last war, by which time TB was no longer a widespread problem, the land was purchased from what was then National Hospitals on a deed of covenant that it was to be a public open space and not to be developed. Admission is therefore free, but a charge is made for car-parking and this allows an estimate to be made of the number of visitors per annum, which was in the region of 80,000 in 1989, 95,000 in 1990.

Thanks to the climate and a south-facing aspect, a great range of plants can be grown here and Simon feels that it could be developed as a quality cultural facility rather than sitting back on the fairground image, which is its present tendency. There are 23 acres, running in some depth behind cliff-tops above the sea.

Hillier's nurseries are near by, and in 1970 Harold Hillier started to supply these gardens, for free, with rare shrubs (rarity value is about the only asset of many of them) of doubtful hardiness in return for being allowed to use them as stock plants for propagation. Whenever gaps appeared, he filled them. On his death, this arrangement came to an end; it did not, in any case, help to create a pleasing garden.

The Goodenoughs, employed by South Wight Borough Council, arrived late in 1986 and in October 1987 were faced with the devastations of the great storm (which totally missed the south-west). Clearing up cost £67,000 and was paid for by various grants and contributions, but there was no budget for reinstatement. The January 1990 storm took two months out of the work programme and cost £7,000; there was no outside help this time. But at the end of it, the garden is much improved!

Money has always been tight, but donations from individuals and small groups have been generous and exceed the budget from the Council by three times. It is a curious locality, inasmuch as many people retire here and can afford to pay prices for their homes which young people cannot, so there is a considerable imbalance in age groups.

The first feature that hits your eye on arrival is a twin-skin polycarbonate, curvilinear temperate house. In case that doesn't quite complete the picture, it looks, when lit up at night, like a jelly mould. Unfortunately the lighting is white; it should be in a range of lurid colours gradually changing in sequence. It would be interesting to see how the plants responded to that.

This feature, conceived by the borough architect, was installed before Simon Goodenough's arrival. It is translucent and plants grow well in it, but it is opaque. The public can't see in from outside but can go in if they pay. No side vents were installed, as these would have enabled the public to take an unpaid-for peek. This means that temperatures rise to undesirable levels in summer. I hope the plants understand that this is in a good cause.

This conservatory is well laid out, the plants grouped in geographical areas (as is fashionable), and attention is paid to annuals, herbaceous perennials and bulbs as well as to shrubs.

Beyond the conservatory is a back-up area with good solid cold frames, built by Simon and two Youth Training Scheme teenagers with 4-inch-thick concrete blocks; and a modern propagation house with mobile benches and a concrete floor (replacing mud). There is also a nitric acid injector to increase the acidity of the water supply, which is excessively alkaline.

In front of the conservatory is a pleasing feature consisting of raised troughs, I would call them, but Simon calls them planters, curved and built at two levels, of nicely rendered and cemented stone, the walls being finished off with a coping on top. These are furnished with a range of colourful plants and when they have a good scent, like the pinks and the bright yellow pea flowers of *Coronilla valentina*, they are handy for your nose.

The blue-daisied *Felicia amelloides* 'Santa Anita' will often come through the winter, though it is quickly replaced if it does not. The bright magenta pink *Cistus* × *purpureus* was already flowering in mid-May, and that has a spicy aroma from stems and leaves. *Gilia tricolor*, an annual that had clearly settled in the previous year, was charming, and a mass of mauve and white flowers like an old-fashioned cotton print frock. *Gypsophila repens* 'Rose Beauty' was making a 4-inch-high mat of pink blossom. The free drainage suited *Convolvulus cneorum*, with silver-grey leaves and white funnel flowers, as also *Salvia argentea*, with large silky white foliage in rosettes, and the shrubby *S. interrupta*, which throws up 4-foot stems of purple flowers above an 18-inch-tall bush.

More of these planters are being set up along the north side of the car-park, which has a cliff behind it.

A few steps take you down to the next terrace level, but as you descend you can hardly miss *Geranium maderense*, on your left, colonizing this steep, sunny bank. It is, for most of us, a tender species. Its deeply cut leaves make it a handsome plant, even without flowers, and it develops a stout trunk, up to 2 feet high. As they die, the leaf petioles bend back on themselves, like tent guy-ropes, until they are touching the ground. In this way the plant, which has to be resistant to salt-laden gales, is firmly held in place. These old leaf-stalks could look scrawny were the older, flowering plants not surrounded, at a lower level, by the greenery of self-sown seedlings.

Flowering will only occur if the plant has a generous root run, so it will never flower under glass unless provided with a large container or planted in the ground. When it flowers, over a long spring and early summer period, it

An amazing colony of *Geranium maderense*, tender in most of Britain.

is abundant with its magenta blossom and its seeds are ejected to a considerable distance. This is the king of cranesbills.

The broad, open terrace we have now reached is uncluttered by trees and gives a sense of freedom and elation. Simon calls it the Mediterranean terrace garden. In its hospital days it was the site of allotments and fruit-growing. The depth of soil is extremely thin, sometimes non-existent, where rock rises above the surface, but that in itself is pleasing to see. If I had a *natural* rock garden I should be an enthusiast for the genre.

Melianthus major was flowering here, which it can only do if its old growth is not frosted. The flowers are curious, not beautiful, and it is best, if winter doesn't perform the job for you, to cut your plants back to the ground or near it each spring. Then you have a foliage plant of unmatched beauty, with large, glaucous, pinnate leaves, heavily toothed. This feature achieves particular depth in early morning or evening sunshine when the leaves cast toothy shadows, one against the next.

Euphorbia mellifera was also flowering. This, again, looks best on its non-flowering leafy shoots. The flowers are nothing to look at but must be retained for the sake of the strong honey fragrance which they waft on the air.

Cytisus canariensis (*Genista fragrans*), with its multitudes of yellow, pea-flowered spikelets, is another shrub that sends out great gusts of welcoming scent. Normally grown as a pot plant, it will make a large shrub, near the sea, until a killer winter overtakes it. After making vigorous growth throughout the summer, it will carry a very worthwhile second flowering through the autumn months.

In the Mediterranean Garden, *Cistus × skanbergii* and *Genista lydia* are strengthened by the sword leaves of a nearby phormium.

Cistuses and brooms are both ideal for this hungry, sun-baked situation and I liked the combination of big, hummocky *Cistus × skanbergii*, covered in pale pink blossom, next to the bright yellow of *Genista lydia*, a broom with stiff, arching sickle branches. Both these shrubs have small leaves and are short on structure, so it was a good idea to have the bold foliage of a New Zealand phormium near by.

In all, there are a lot of phormiums, which have been so much developed for their colourful foliage in recent years. In one area there is an intentional concentration of New Zealand flora. Although they both have strap leaves, they differed so markedly in colouring and texture that it looked good to see the silver-grey *Astelia chathamica* (I can't have too much of that) in front of a dark-leaved phormium and a pseudopanax behind them, with glossy palmate leaves. You see a lot of them in New Zealand.

Griselinia littoralis is a New Zealand native, with thick-textured, soap-smooth ovate leaves of a bright, cheerful green at all seasons. This is a common seaside windbreak shrub but I had not met *G. lucida* before. Its leaves are much larger and very glossy.

The New Zealand kowhai, their national flower, was represented by a particularly showy form, *Sophora microphylla* 'Goldilocks' (rather a banal name, surely), with large bell-shaped pea flowers in the usual clusters and of a strong yellow.

I had not realized what a sight *Cordyline australis*, grown mainly for the exotic appearance of its long strap leaves, borne in rosettes on a shrub that eventually becomes a tree, can be when flowering. It carries voluptuously branching panicles of white star flowers in prodigal abundance and their scent on the air is wonderful.

Having walked a little way eastwards along this terrace we came to a herb garden, well placed for being near the restaurant and also for the thin soil that pleases herbs. I liked the juxtaposition of French lavender, *Lavandula stoechas*, waving its purple flags, and the bright young foliage of golden marjoram. That would probably scorch, later on, in such an open situation, but if you then shear it over it will flush again.

The restaurant, called the Tavern, was a workshop to the hospital and there were dairies and piggeries around here. There is plenty of space for people to eat *al fresco* and we did. However, the formally laid-out garden in front of the Tavern is rather awful. Simon has got rid of most of the hideous Hybrid Tea and Floribunda rose bushes (being called a despoiler of English beauty by one irate gentleman), but there remains the central pond and its raised concrete surround, done on the cheap and really tawdry.

You are very much aware of the quantities of long teak seats in this area, though they abound throughout the garden. They wouldn't look so obtrusive if they were allowed to weather and bleach to grey. Simon tried this, one year, holding off the linseed oil, but was immediately hauled up by touchy presenters of these memorials to their dear departed.

Those that were not inscribed were got rid of and an embargo was placed on new presentations. That made Simon unpopular but he can take it. A superabundance of seats in a garden mars its appearance.

Close to the Tavern is the Palm Garden, with *Trachycarpus fortunei*, many of which date back to hospital days. Cannas grow here as hardy plants and were already 2 feet tall on their new shoots.

I remarked on some cables and light-fittings that were at the surface of some of these beds. It seems that they were laid all over the garden, for spot-lighting, at vast expense, and were all vandalized and useless within two years. No irrigation lines were laid, however, despite the site being so dry. Two thirds of the garden now has water available and the supply has not been restricted during droughts although, of course, it is metered.

The great feature in the Palm Garden area is the extraordinary colony of *Echium pininana*. Their scores of 12–14-foot flowering spikes add up to hundreds; ropes of blue flowers interspersed by long, horizontal leafy bracts. Perhaps, like owning a herd of giraffes, this is more exciting than beautiful, but who cares? Normally the possessor of a single flowering *E. pininana* is a proud gardener, but this was beyond belief.

In youth, the self-sown seedlings make a rosette of foliage, close to ground level and a bold feature in itself. This runs up to flower in its third year. The great

Grotesquely compelling: a huge, self-perpetuating colony of *Echium pininana*.

disturbance caused by fallen trees and their removal in 1987 brought a lot of echium seed to the surface and there have been great germinations ever since.

From the garden's most easterly point we looped back westwards via the sea cliffs. This took us first through the disappeared woodland area, which was on the site of the quarry. The trees were ilex, alias holm oak, *Quercus ilex*, an evergreen noted for its tolerance of salt but pretty dismal in its habitually battered appearance. The area looks good now with its expanse of rock and scree. Astelias, planted as tiny offsets only two years previously, had already made clumps 5 feet across.

To make new paths, you have to scratch around for local materials, as haulage from the mainland is so costly. Gravel from a local pit was edged with timbers from old sea defences.

On the sea cliffs there is naturalized (as you see wallflowers elsewhere) a long-lived, single-flowered white stock, listed in *The Plant Finder* as '*Matthiola*

white perennial', and recorded here years ago. It has got around to many gardens, including my own, these past ten years or so. Its scent is just what you expect of a stock. When colonized on a cliff face, up-draughts bear this fragrance to anyone standing on the top, and there is a public footpath here.

Single white stocks are naturalized on the garden's cliff face boundary.

Having returned to the garden's west end, there is a piece of woodland that has survived and the trees are underplanted with colonies of hart's-tongue fern (abundant in the wild on the chalk, hereabouts), stinking hellebore (*Helleborus foetidus*), arum lilies (*Zantedeschia aethiopica*) and columbines from the national collection. They all mix happily together.

The Wall Garden that you're in on your return journey is backed by a high wall (not enclosed by walls) 70 metres long, with a good 5-metre-deep mixed border in front of it. Simon thinks in metres, as we should all be doing, by now, if Thatcher hadn't reneged on metrication in her early days. We're now in an uncomfortable state of suspended metrication.

The border was all Hillier shrubs, and some remain, but the fact of its contents now being mixed has livened it up no end. Salvias do well, and the pineapple-scented *Salvia rutilans* is hardy. The Paris daisy, *Argyranthemum* (once *Chrysanthemum*) *frutescens*, makes a huge billowing white pouffe that comfortably overlaps the frontal lawn edge by several feet. It took Simon three years to teach the Borough Council staff responsible for mowing and edging *not* to keep it trimmed back from the edges. I wonder what proportion of wives have succeeded in training their husbands to let well alone in the same context in private gardening? The division is always a battlefront.

Old, winter-surviving bushes of *Osteospermum* 'Whirligig', with pinched-in white rays opening to spoon ends, went well with the lacy grey foliage of *Artemisia* 'Powis Castle' and, behind them, *Euryops abrotanifolius*, with finely divided, bright green leaves and yellow daisies. This has a flopping habit but the easiest way is to let it flop. It still makes a 3-foot-high bush.

The wall offers good shelter to less hardy plants and there is a vast specimen, dating from 1979, of the evergreen climber, *Trachylospermum jasminoides*, which carries a long succession of heavily scented, cream-coloured (rather dirty cream) flowers similar in appearance to a jasmine's. It belongs, in fact, to the periwinkle family, *Apocynaceae*.

The biennial incense plant (from Australia), *Humea elegans*, had survived the previous mild winter near to the wall. It makes such a handsome pot plant for the conservatory, with its masses of coral-coloured, scented blossom, that it's a shame that seed has become virtually impossible for the amateur to obtain. Admittedly some people are allergic to it and need to handle it with gloves on, but that applies to many popular plants.

From a Brian Mathew collection, the original sweet pea, *Lathyrus odoratus*, from its native Sicily, was flowering in this border. Its scent is amazingly pungent; the flower colour an agreeable indigo violet.

Simon is very careful with the money he can lay hands on, so his policy is to buy one stock plant of anything desirable, after which Deb propagates it on the spot. Seed comes to them from botanic gardens all over the world. All this saves a lot of cash.

This is an impressive enterprise and improving by leaps and bounds all the time. One must hope that the pay is generous enough to keep the Goodenoughs happy here for a few years yet.

POSTSCRIPT

A return visit in mid-July (*quatorze juillet*), three years on, confirms me in the belief that this is one of the most encouragingly progressive gardens in our country. Simon runs it with a staff of only four. Lawns alone take one man three days a week, in the growing season, to mow, and edging has to be done once monthly.

The Palm Garden was particularly voluptuous in high summer, purple-leaved, red-flowered cannas mixing well with blue agapanthus. Many of the agapanthus in these gardens are grown in quite deep shade, and they flower well. Simon took his cue from seeing them like this, beneath camphor trees, in South Africa.

Coral red watsonias were flowering freely in the Palm Garden, huge yuccas likewise, while foliage was making the main contribution – gaudy phormiums, beschornerias, the variegated form of giant reed grass (*Arundo donax*) and a young Chusan palm, which can mix in with others mentioned at a quite low level, before it has developed a trunk. A good case can be made for discarding a proportion of your plants once the tree-like habit begins to develop, and replacing with youngsters, which will probably turn up as self-sowns, anyway. Acanthus tie in with this outfit, and cordylines.

There is a nearby New Zealand section, where I enjoyed the silver-grey *Astelia chathamica* highlighted by a purple-leaved phormium behind it. Thus a similarity in habit but a contrast in colour. Grasses are normally better kept apart; too many grass leaves together are apt to look messy. But if the contrast in other respects is sufficient, they can make good partners. Here, bold clumps of toe-toe, the New Zealand version of pampas grass, *Cortaderia richardii*, was making big, free-flowering clumps behind quite low domes of *Stipa arundinacea*, a shimmering grass, soft pink on its young inflorescences.

The Ventnor Botanic Garden should be visited frequently, not merely through the seasons but to watch its progress from year to year.

PPS

The latest news is not good. The two Wight Councils have amalgamated (which is sensible) but as reconstituted the grant to the gardens, for which they are responsible, has been cut by twenty per cent. This is depressing for Simon and Deb. If they moved elsewhere, the gardens would suffer and the Council would have themselves to blame.

STREAM COTTAGE

———❦———

I FIRST VISITED Stream Cottage, near Fittleworth in West Sussex (my own
county but a couple of exasperating hours' driving from home), in the
middle of just about the hottest day of the year. I was with Fergus Garrett
and we were at the start of one of our garden-visiting forays into Dorset.
Delighted by the place and its owner, we went again the following summer.
Hot weather suits the garden perfectly. A high sun fills the glades with light
but there is much relief in the shade of trees and shrubs.

Stream Cottage is a single-storey building, built around 1600, where octo-
genarian Peter Addington lives on his own. Of wiry build, he still seems to
get through an amazing amount of work and gardening has been in his blood
from early youth; he had the advantage of a bevy of gardening aunts. As the
cottage lies in a shallow valley right at the end of a small lane, there is virtually
no parking space for cars, let alone coaches, so the garden cannot be opened
to the public, though prearranged visits by specialist groups do sometimes
occur.

Peter is best known as a bamboo expert and he was President of the
Bamboo Society for a number of years. He holds the National Collection of
phyllostachys, which I consider to be the most valuable ornamental genus of
all bamboos. It has great style, still looks reasonably presentable after the
ravages of winter (which is more than can be said of most evergreens) and
does not run about inconveniently in our climate (though it can do where
summers are warmer and moister).

But the great thing about Peter is that he is no specialist. Any plant may
have an appeal for him. What's more, he not merely understands how to get
the best out of a plant, culturally, but he also has a keen eye for presenting it
attractively and in the best of company. Although the bamboos are numerous,
you don't immediately have premonitions of bamboo indigestion. They are
cunningly woven into the garden fabric, with other shrubs and plants assuming
no less important roles. I imagine that secateurs are seldom out of his hands

and he has a knack for trimming shrubs, sometimes because this is the best way to accommodate them within limited space, but sometimes, also, because an imposed shape appears more flatteringly than the natural.

He loves variegated plants, and in the small front garden on the south side of the cottage is the frantically variegated *Deutzia scabra* 'Punctata', with a speckling of green dots over a white ground. This is trimmed to a height of 3 feet, and a tendency to reversion to plain green is condoned on a proportion of shoots, since a bit of green highlights the variegation. By the same token, of course, variegated plants are not grown side by side but are highlighted by plain-leaved kinds.

A little path has been made through this colony of *Chusquea breviglumis*, which is much thinned to give the feeling of space.

Visitors to Inverewe, in north-west Scotland, are generally impressed by the white-variegated Turkish oak tree, *Quercus cerris* 'Argenteovariegata', just across a lawn from the house, but at Stream Cottage this also looks pleasing and lively trimmed to remain a shrub.

Against the cottage's warm south wall grow both species of the evergreen twining climber, *Trachelospermum*. Both have waxy, cream-coloured, jasmine-like flowers, scented on the air, though the scents are different. Peter finds that *T. asiaticum* flowers the more freely. *T. jasminoides wilsonii* tends to flower on the young growth. Its leaves turn reddish purple in winter. There was a newly emerged Comma butterfly feeding on the blossom.

High against the gable end, a splendid *Itea ilicifolia*. Its shiny evergreen leaves have the crisp texture of stiff paper. Long racemes of tiny green flowers, lemon-scented at night, come out in August. This has been likened to *Garrya elliptica*, though that will take a north wall and flowers in January. Its leaves are far coarser and make a dull summer feature.

There is a lovely, virile specimen, in this front garden, of a lime green form of the Korean fir, *Abies koreana*, a slenderly tapering spire. It cones a little, not generously as do some strains of the type plant. The New Zealand wire netting plant, *Corokia cotoneaster*, can look a scruffy object (it does in my garden), but Peter's is the finest specimen I've ever seen and should make one resolve to give it its best chance. The slender branchlets twist all over the place; the tiny spoon-shaped leaves are evergreen. In May, the shrub covers itself with little yellow star flowers and they can be charming.

By Peter Addington's front door, a seedling of *Fargesia murieliae* (more familiar as *Arundinaria murieliae*) makes a beautiful pot specimen, with feathery growth. This would never work were it a division from a mature plant, which would produce coarse, dominant canes (culms, to bamboo *aficionados*).

Growing bamboos in roomy pots is a great idea. When looking their best, they can be stood in key positions, on paving, where there's no ground to grow things in. When tatty, they can be removed from the scene to a backup area or, if tender, to a greenhouse, for the winter. So it is with the Mexican *Chusquea coronalis*, which is not in the least hardy and looks its worst in spring. But in summer and autumn it is light and feathery, with its small, narrow leaves. *C. ramosissima* is a true climber with attractive, arching canes. It is not quite hardy but a good pot plant.

Another pot-grown favourite is *Chimonobambusa tumidissinoda* (bamboo names are not calculated to popularize them, especially as they keep on being changed). This can be grown in the ground, where it runs around a little but is easily controlled (all bamboo enthusiasts will say that of their favourites, whether true or not). It'll reach only 5 feet in as many years and is fresh green

with a graceful habit. The closely set nodes are conspicuously inflated and in China it is used to make walking-sticks.

Peter repots most of his pot-grown bamboos every year in a peat-based compost supplied him by David Crampton, whose Hampshire nursery specializes in bamboos, and there are sufficient slow-acting nutrients in this for further feeding to be unnecessary during the growing season. Repotting also includes splitting, in most cases, and is done in spring.

Of the best-known chusquea, *C. culeou*, from Chile, it is interesting to learn that seedlings can be divided quite easily. If planted deeply in a pot, the submerged nodes will make roots and can thereafter be cut apart and treated separately. From adult colonies, propagation is cumbersome by divisions and uncertain. The densely tufted branching from closely set nodes in this species, gives it a brush-like appearance, growth being pretty stiff. I have it as a lawn specimen and you certainly cannot miss it. Seedlings are extremely variable in height, vigour, hardiness and other aspects.

Near to the greenhouse, every plant is of interest. In a bit of paving, the

Cornus alternifolia 'Argentea', with its elegant foliage and tiered habit of growth, makes a point of interest in a pre-eminent position.

cracks and margins are colonized by the near-black *Ophiopogon planiscapus* 'Nigrescens', whose dark colouring and strap leaves are contrasted with the heart leaves of the golden dead nettle, *Lamium maculatum* 'Aureum'. There is also a strange violet species, sometimes called tree violet, *Viola elatior*, with washy pale blue flowers on a tall, sparse plant. That self-sows.

In complete contrast is a dense 20-foot colony of *Phyllostachys sulphurea* 'Robert Young', with magnificent, thick canes. However, it, like many other bamboos, does shed a lot of leaves and sheaths in the summer, so it isn't easy to underplant close to them. A tall bamboo of stiffish habit that keeps itself to itself, it is especially useful for making a fast-growing boundary barrier – an excellent change from Leyland cypress and a lot more imaginative. Of similar height and upright habit is *Semiarundinaria fastuosa*, 'Viridis' being the best clone with greener canes and leaves. I have now planted that at the back of a border where I don't want it to encroach on its neighbours. Perhaps it won't, for a while.

If I jump from bamboos to completely different plants and back to bamboos again, that's the way it is in this garden. I had always thought of *Abelia schumannii* as being too tender for ordinary border uses, but its tubular flowers are of a more definite shade of pink than those of the hardy *A. grandiflora*. Here, in a frost hollow, it is a large and long-established bush, flowering all summer. I have planted one and it seems to be taking off. I hadn't met *Sarcococca saligna* before and it is a good 3-foot evergreen foliage shrub for year-round effect, with long lance leaves of fresh green colouring. Unlike most sarcococcas, the flowers have no scent.

The maple-like foliage of *Kirengeshoma palmata* contrasts with *Astilbe chinensis pumila* in a glade at Stream Cottage.

On both my visits I was taken by a small, scrambling evergreen bramble, *Rubus ichangensis*. Its stems, thickly set with small, hooked prickles, are a feature in themselves, while the lance leaves, cordate at the base, have an attractive pale sheen. Its growth is none too hardy but this doesn't matter because, as with all brambles grown for their foliage, it is best to cut everything back to the ground each spring.

A beautiful mature *Cornus alternifolia* 'Argentea' has now reached its full height of 15 feet and shimmers seductively with light, airy foliage, more white than green.

An area of lawn, longer than broad, leads you down the garden and is flanked by massive plantings. There are trees – some of them mature sweet chestnuts – on the concealed boundaries, so nothing seems finite. The pale green, soap-smooth oval leaves of *Griselinia littoralis* make a handsome contrasting background for a variegated aucuba. Peter is no despiser of spotted laurels, but you need to pick and choose the best. Variegated foliage also contrasts well with bamboo. Thus, *Elaeagnus* × *ebbingei* 'Limelight' by the side of a 25-foot *Phyllostachys rubromarginata*, of narrow habit, red-edged cane sheaths giving it its name.

Peter has quite a large collection of osmanthus. Most of us know and grow only *O. delavayi* and *O.* × *burkwoodii* for their scented spring flowers, with, perhaps, the holly-leaved *O. heterophyllus* for the autumn. Here I saw *O. serrulatus*, a vigorous evergreen with quite big leaves, 5 inches long and having small marginal teeth. Its flowers are almond-scented in spring. Peter collected the seed from Mount Omei in 1971, when on an expedition with Roy Lancaster.

I cannot really see much virtue in the allspice, *Calycanthus occidentalis*, making as it does a large, loose shrub with coarse leaves and spangled only here and there (though over a long season) with its dusky red flowers. Perhaps its main talking point is that they smell of sour wine. But, near to ground level, I liked the combination of two shade- and moisture-loving (the soil never dries out, here) perennials: *Kirengeshoma palmata*, with its maple-like leaves, dark stems and pale yellow shuttlecock flowers, behind the stiff, bright mauve panicles of *Astilbe chinensis pumila*.

Here's a good, vigorous bamboo, only 4 feet tall, though slightly invasive (nothing to worry about!) – I'm growing it in a container: *Pleioblastus shibuyanus* 'Tsuboi'. Tsuboi seems to be the word to hang on to. The broadish leaves have bright white striations (variegated bamboos can usually be best seen if looked down on) and remain in excellent condition to winter's end. Peter clips it over a bit in spring, so that it makes a roundish bush.

The lower end of the lawn is cut off from the remaining, wilder, area, from

The graceful arching branches of Muriel Wilson's bamboo (*Fargesia murieliae*) make a calculated contrast to ferns and large-leaved hostas.

which all grass paths have been eliminated, replacing them with bark, which also forms mulches everywhere, by a 4-foot brick wall. Naturally you can see over this. An interestingly planted border in front has a 15-inch-tall colonizing fern, with elegant, bipinnate fronds, in front of a hummock of *Rhododendron yakushimanum*, so good for its glaucous foliage, especially when young. Ferns are as ill-served in their names as bamboos. This one, introduced by Dr Alan Leslie, is *Pseudophegopteris levingei*. A purple Jackman clematis tumbles over the wall and has the golden bamboo, *Pleioblastus (Arundinaria) auricoma* in front of it – a good contrast. There is another itea, here. To the left of the wall is an interesting bamboo, more interesting, in fact, than beautiful. This is *Chusquea quila*, which grows wild on forest margins along the borders of Chile and Argentina. Its long, willowy canes define the habit of climbing into trees. Peter has provided it with *Hydrangea heteromalla*, through and over which to do this. It is just about the largest-growing species in this genus, but I have my doubts on whether the bamboo may not beat it to the finishing post.

A low-growing golden bamboo is saved from sun scorch by taller shrubs and trees close by.

Over the wall, you admire the great arching plumes of *Chusquea breviglumis*. It was known as *C. culeou tenuis*, which grows to 3–4 feet only. It is reaching 20 feet in height by as much across and is the largest of its kind in Europe. Peter Addington sees to it that every plant in his garden is well nourished and grows extremely well. On rounding the end of the wall, you find yourself in front of this bamboo's well-spaced (because thinned out) canes, with a path and stepping stones leading through the centre of the colony. It is a wonderful sight, attained by hard work. Peter does a great deal of cane thinning through-out his garden. Those that remain are all the better displayed.

Ferns associate well with bamboos and, at a higher level, so do conifers. Thus, *Sciadopitys verticillata*, which makes a large tree-shrub in time, furnished to the ground. Its leaves (they are a little too broad to be called needles, but not much) are arranged in whorls at regular intervals along the shoots. I know of no other plant with a stronger identity. Then there is *Cunninghamia lanceolata*, with rather broad, sharp-tipped lance leaves and a bright pale green colouring. Solid and static, it is in the centre of a glade surrounded by phyllostachys. Normally, I rather dislike this conifer, which has the unpleasant habit of retaining its old, dead leaves long after they have browned. That was not the case here. Doubtless Peter had been busy.

Some notable bamboos include *Thamnocalamus crassinodus* 'Kew Beauty' and a similar, though superior, clone called 'Merlyn' (after Merlyn Edwards, who brought seedlings back from the Langtan valley in Bhutan). It makes upright clumps to 15 feet, clothed with very fine, narrow leaves that create a mist of green. New canes are covered in a powdering of soft blue.

Peter has enviably thick canes on his *Phyllostachys bambusoides* 'Castillonis'. It needs moisture and nourishment for this, and I realize that mine will never achieve this strength, situated as it is in an old meadow/orchard and surrounded by competitive turf. This bamboo is handsomest on its young canes, when they are bright yellow with a similarly bright green flash on the flat side of each internode. In *P. b.* 'Castillonis Inversa', also grown here, the principal cane colouring is green, while the flat area is yellow.

More frivolous elements in this area are provided by the evergreen buck-thorn, *Rhamnus alaternus* 'Variegatus' (a favourite of mine, too), which is clipped over, and by a dwarfened elder in which many leaves are spun out to fine threads. This is *Sambucus nigra* 'Linearis'; it has a bamboo-like quality. Peter is also very good at finding low plants which reflect such sky light as reaches them beneath so much of shade. Thus, the dwarf, colonizing subspecies of *Daphne laureola* called *philippi* (native of the Pyrenees), with rosettes of dark green leaves, was looking really healthy. The bugle, *Ajuga reptans* 'Catlin's Giant', with substantial, shining purple leaves, induced me to buy one at considerable cost at Wisley, a few weeks later. An evergreen fern, *Dryopteris braunii*, has an almost metallic lustre on its dark green fronds.

There is a boggy bit with a range of happy ferns, generally selections aberrant from familiar species. Thus the royal fern, *Osmunda regalis*, is re-presented by 'Crispa', with wavy-margined pinnules, and 'Cristata', which is crested. The delightful sensitive fern, *Onoclea sensibilis*, so fresh in spring but with an uninhibited running habit, is represented by a form in which the young fronds and rachis are rosy copper. The hardy maidenhair fern, *Adiantum pedatum*, whose pinnae are arranged like spokes around a semicircular base, looks good beneath an unusually strong example of *Rodgersia pinnata* 'Superba', whose rugged, palmate leaves are exceptionally rich purplish bronze, when young. The fresh green discs of *R. tabularis*, as we knew it, now *Astilboides tabularis*, also makes a colony, here. The white-flowered aroid, *Arisaema candidissima*, with broadly trifoliate leaves, has also established well, so there is much contrast at a lowish level in foliage colour and form.

A big American river birch, *Betula nigra*, and a massive colony of *Pleioblastus linearis*, with long, narrow leaves, bring this garden to a close, and still you're unaware of neighbours, though they do exist.

There's another, intimate, area for sitting out and contemplation, on the north side of the cottage, which I should have liked to include, but I shall not. Enough is enough and I hope I have succeeded in showing that this is the best sort of individual garden, achieved through a passion for plants and realized by a combination of good taste and expertise.

COLDHAM

———⟫-◦-⟪———

OLDHAM, overlooking a large, traditional cricket green at Little Chart Forstal, is in one of the few remaining unspoilt parts of Kent – at the time of writing, that is, and with reservations, which include the hum of the M20 motorway. The trouble for Kent is that it has London on one side and the nearest entry from the Continent on the other. Any unspoilt bits will be the cheapest through which to run a new motorway, railway, electricity or gas line, or to set up an aerodrome, so threats are continual, harassing and expensive to combat.

Still, there they are and have been for many years, Dr Jack and Jean Elliott, he a physician who retired early and has since devoted himself to gardening, serving the Royal Horticultural Society in many ways, notably on Council. His first and, probably still, foremost love is for alpines, but he loves all sorts of plants, hardy or tender (he has quite a bit of glass), trees, shrubs, herbaceous perennials. He travels in many parts of the world, lecturing, picking up new plants, but is also a great sharer; together with Maurice Mason, one of the most generous I have met.

Above all, Jack is a collector and cultivator. He knows about display, but that doesn't come first with him. He likes the details of flowers and enjoys the sort which only yield their innermost secrets through a magnifying glass. His garden is excellently kept but always in an exuberant state of flux, so what I write about that I noted a few years ago has probably changed since then and will have changed still more by the time this is published. You do see good plant combinations at Coldham but they are probably accidental and will almost certainly disappear by the next season.

The largest-flowered hardy honeysuckle, *Lonicera tragophylla*, is beautiful but wears no perfume. Evening primrose and scabious in foreground.

The garden covers, I suppose, an acre or two, and the land around here is flat. That made the vertical feature of a gigantic Lombardy poplar immensely important. You might think that a vertical of that kind took up no more space than the girth of its trunk, but that would be to ignore its roots. Jack and Jean loathed the thing and, against my strict injunctions, removed it, making space for flowering cherries and suchlike frippery. I have never forgiven or forgotten, even after twenty years. (It might, admittedly, have blown down in one of the two subsequent storms – or it might not.)

The garden has a surprising number of ragstone walls and, what with an extra wing, you are three parts into a courtyard at the house entrance, much of it shaded by the house. There is a pump in the middle of paving and lots of self-seeding *Alchemilla mollis* in the cracks. Just the right place for it, where it can't muscle out anything less robust. Shade suited the largest specimen of *Daphne pontica* that I have ever seen. Such a handsome shrub, with its rosettes of glossy, evergreen foliage, to which it adds a seething mass of clustered, pale green blossom, deliciously night-scented of lemon, on the air, each May. It suffered badly in one of the stinking winters of the 1980s, recovered completely but seems now to be faltering. You can't expect a daphne to last for ever. (STOP PRESS: It died.)

Helleborus argutifolius is robustly healthy in this bed, and *Mahonia nervosa*, from Oregon, a low-growing, suckering species with long, pinnate leaves of a particularly smart cut. It isn't an easy plant in the south-east but can clearly be a success if you try hard enough to please it (I didn't). Jack has the fashionable new *Choisya* 'Aztec Pearl' doing well for him and the best-selling *C. ternata* 'Sundance' looking, I have to say, healthier than I have yet seen it (except immediately after planting out) in any garden. It has been the garden centre's dream come true because, when raised under protection, its prettily shaped leaves and tender yellow-green colouring are irresistible, but once exposed to the blasts of real life out of doors, it becomes a truly sickly object. However, here it seems to have just the degree of protection and of shade to suit it.

Most of the beds in this front garden (and many elsewhere) are raised, which provides extra good drainage. × *Halimiocistus wintonensis* appreciates that. It carries a long succession of white flowers (yellow at the centre), with ultra-large maroon blotches. Its habit is scrawny. I don't know if that could be helped by some pinching back in its earlier days.

The true *Lonicera tragophylla*, which has pure yellow flowers but is often confused with *L.* × *tellmanniana*, grows on a wall that's shaded till afternoon. Apparently it comes quite easily from seed (cuttings are not too amenable), but would, I suppose, cross rather too readily with other honeysuckles in the garden. Of the hardy species, this has the largest flowers and you can easily forgive it for not being scented.

There's a colony of the white, grey-leaved Californian tree poppy, *Romneya coulteri*, near the garage. To the right is a tall bush of *Bupleurum fruticosum*, the only shrubby member of *Umbelliferae* that one ever meets; a plant with great style and free with its compound umbels of green flowers. This had to be moved when it grew so large that the car could no longer find an exit from the garage, but there are two promising self-sown seedlings (some people have all the luck), 'slightly better placed', Jack claims. I wonder how many years 'slightly' will give them in their self-appointed positions.

The shrubby, summer-flowering *Jasminum humile revolutum* is apt to carry its clusters of yellow flowers over too long a season for them to make much impact at any one time, but Jack's one is pretty powerful. A marvellous clump of *Euphorbia rigida* grows at its feet. Such a good foliage plant with its sharply pointed, glaucous leaves, as effective in winter as at any season. But its terminal clusters of lime green flowers in February and March are also most welcome in the years when they put in an appearance. It is not altogether hardy, but this again is on a raised level and I'm sure Jack would always hold spare stock in reserve. He is a compulsive propagator and surplus stock is sold (at much too low prices) on days when the garden is open for charity.

He is very keen on the genus *Euphorbia* altogether. The honey-scented *E. mellifera* grows very tall against a sheltered wall near by. Probably it is best given a fairly heavy pruning after having flowered, to keep it shapely, especially as the foliage borne on young stems is its handsomest feature. The flowers are nothing to look at but exhale the scent. Right on the other side of the garden,

The Great White Cherry, 'Tai Haku', was rediscovered by Collingwood ('Cherry') Ingram in Japan. *Euphorbia characias* spp. *wulfenii* self-sows freely in this garden.

in an area with the feel of woodland, is a large, self-seeding colony of the shrubby *E. characias*, up to 7 feet tall.

Then he has a delightful, smallish shrubby species (which he has twice given me and I'm hopeful of being more successful with it the second time), the Turkish *E. macrostegia*. Its rosettes of leaves are wavy-edged and highly polished. The green inflorescence turns pink with age if in a sufficiently sunny position. And the herbaceous, 2-foot *E. ceratocarpa*, in which the most notable feature, when you look at the plant as a whole, is the sharp, acute angle made by each bract in the inflorescence.

I don't suppose he collects them intentionally, but Jack also seems to have a penchant for peas, *Lathyrus*. He always grows some of the wild sweet pea, *L. odoratus*, originating in Sicily and with much the strongest perfume. Then he has a fairly strident magenta form of the herbaceous, perennial pea, *L. latifolius*, growing through *Clematis orientalis*, with thick-sepalled yellow lanterns, the form introduced by Ludlow & Sheriff. I liked that combination just as much as the pure white form of the same pea species running through the purple-leaved vine, *Vitis vinifera* 'Purpurea'. In a mixed border he has a huge mound, much the most vigorous colony I have seen, of the bricky red *L. rotundifolius*.

Past the garage you come to a cul-de-sac with a greenhouse in its centre and a sun frame running parallel alongside it, though with an alley between. The sun frame is raised so that you can see into it and work at it easily and without stooping. It is filled with special well-draining compost and can be covered with glass in winter to prevent the kind of alpines that can all too easily moulder away in our climate from getting too wet. A sun frame is not a beautiful garden feature; far from it, but it looked far worse in the old days when filled with bright terracotta-coloured plastic pots, each the home of a precious *Fritillaria* species. There are no pots here any longer and the bed has been landscaped a bit with rocks and contains some good cushion-forming plants; for instance *Phlox nana* 'Arroya', which is shocking magenta, and 'Tangelo', which is orange. Both are Mexican. From the Atlas mountains, *Delphinium balansae* makes a mat, which is unusual in this genus, and it is free with its blue flowers.

In a trough at the end of the greenhouse is the late-flowering, mat-forming *Campanula waldsteiniana*, with upturned chalices opening into stars on the pointed lobes, in campanula blue. What a genus. The interior of this greenhouse seldom detains one for long but on its other side, in the shade, is another raised border full of peaty soil, the happy home of *Erythronium revolutum*, haberleas, ramondas, hardy orchids, notably an American helleborine, *Epipactis gigantea*, with brownish green flowers. It is a nice fresh-looking plant that runs about.

A south-facing mixed border in summer.

On the sunny side of this cul-de-sac are unnamed alstroemerias from seed collected in the Andes, one of them a soft, burnt orange that appealed to me. *Asphodeline brevicaulis* is like *A. liburnica* in opening its greeny yellow stars quite late in the afternoon, for an evening display, but its foliage is coarser. It grows to $3\frac{1}{2}$ feet. *Zauschneria septemtrionalis* is mat-forming with grey-green leaves. It has a nice habit and is brilliant with red, tubular flowers in late summer and autumn.

Jack is tempted by a number of tender or half-hardy plants. A gazania called 'Slate' is unusual, with grey leaves and purple flowers, each ray edged in cream. He gave me cuttings and, at the time of writing, in March, I think some of my plants have survived the winter outside. He was growing *Nemesia fruticans* with the 'Hidcote Purple' bedding verbena and *Lavatera maritima* (more descriptively known as *L. bicolor*) behind them. The nemesia, going through a range of name changes, has come into our gardens only recently and is mauve, easily struck from cuttings and a good bedder, though needing to be shorn over half-way through the season to start it off again. The mallow is a fast-growing shrub with attractive grey-green leaves and pale mauve flowers with a purple centre. Young plants are apt to smother their flowers in foliage. If you can bring your plant through the winter, the balance is better in its second year.

Another malvaceous plant that Jack grows most successfully against a warm wall, where it can bring its old growth through the winter, is *Malvastrum lateritium*. That has salmon-coloured flowers and they are much too scattered

The tall *Papaver orientale* (Goliath Group) 'Beauty of Livermere' behind the dwarf, double, freely suckering poppy 'Fireball'.

to be effective if the plants (which are hardy enough) have to start again each spring from ground level, but prolific on old shoots that survived. *Osteospermum* 'Silver Sparkler' lives up to its name with shimmering green and white foliage, the daisies being blue and white. At Coldham it seems to keep on flowering well through the summer, though many of these osteospermums go into a summer recess.

I wish I did *Lobelia laxiflora angustifolia* better. The plant is hardy enough but it really needs to bring its old growth, which is a foot tall and evergreen, intact through the winter if it is to flower freely. On the young shoots, flowering is sparse at best. Jack's was flowering well on its old wood. A really warm position is indicated. The flowers are tubular, coral red on the outside, cream yellow within. *Euryops pectinatus* is hardy in the Isle of Wight but not for most of us. A fast-growing shrub with handsome, grey pinnate foliage, it puts on a display of penetratingly clear yellow daisies in spring.

Turning from the small and tender to the large and hardy, Jack has good shrubs and trees. The ultra-silvery *Salix exigua* is obviously very much at home and runs about suckering like mad. Not many willows behave like that and I shouldn't say it was a menace. For some years, now, he has grown the pink variegated form of box elder, *Acer negundo* 'Flamingo', and it hasn't gone into a middle-aged decline. It responds well to being headed back and can be treated as an easily controllable shrub. I think *Pyrus* is an underrated genus for ornamental purposes and forgetting about edible pears. *P. salicifolia* 'Pendula' is all too well known and widely planted but *P. nivalis* is a good tree of upright habit, grey-green leaves and freely flowering. I also liked the look of *Sorbus*

Pots containing *Bidens ferulifolia* (left) and *Cuphea ceciliae* (centre).

koehneana, a large shrub rather than a small tree, with pretty, pinnate leaves and trusses of pure white berries.

Barberries are not often endearing, but the deciduous *Berberis prattii laxipendula* is an excellent late-flowering shrub, with 9-inch long branching panicles of yellow blossom, followed by no less attractive fruits in autumn. For years, now, Coldham has had a tremendously heavily cropping specimen of the silver fir, *Abies koreana*, which often cones as quite a baby. *Abies* cones are always held so importantly, like candles on the upper sides of horizontal branches. The overall ground colouring of these cones is grey-blue, but each scale has a tongue-like bract poking out at its base, pale green and arranged in spirals – a beautiful construction. This tree became so wide at the base that it was becoming impossible to pass by it on either side, so the lower branches were removed. I thought it would never recover its poise and balance, but it has.

Looking out from the drawing-room window, double mixed borders flank the view and these used to be filled with roses. They looked a fright, as rose beds always do, and Jack got rid of them but could not immediately replant because of the residual herbicide that had been used among the bushes. Now he keeps the plantings to colours that exclude red, yellow and orange, these being located elsewhere. That includes a most daring planting with which I will conclude what could otherwise become a list of plants. The scarlet *Lychnis* × *arkwrightii* is growing next to the brilliant reddish purple, almost magenta, *Geranium* 'Ann Folkard'.

At least they were together and I hope they still are, but you know how things change and I have to say: it's best that they should, keeping us young of mind. I hope they'll be planting a young Lombardy poplar soon.

THE BETH CHATTO GARDENS

—▸◦◂—

ETH CHATTO'S name has attained such star quality among gardeners in the past thirty years that it is a little daunting to attempt a summary of her achievement. Fortunately I need only to approach the subject tangentially, here, not being directly concerned with her nursery or with her writings, except in so far as they have been influenced by her garden and vice versa.

Beth is an old friend. We not only visit each other but have travelled together, both on holiday and lecturing, the latter taking us around the world. This makes it a little difficult to get my subject into perspective.

She is a great proselytizer and a great teacher and she teaches by example, giving the world ample opportunities to profit from her abundant and evident creativity. She did not start out as a gardener, though she waded into garden-making from the earliest days of her marriage. Her husband was a fruit farmer; fruit farming fell on difficult times and only the most dedicated persisted. Beth saw that some other way had to be found in order to survive. Already recognized locally as a collector of unusual plants, she was invited to be a founder member of Colchester Flower Club and still shines in the art of flower-arranging (in which her style has none of the pretentious artificiality so often met with among flower arrangers today). She made a garden for the Essex home that was built specially for them, next to the fruit; she learned to propagate her own plants, as amateurs do, when they want to save on purchases, and in any case the techniques of propagation are among the most exciting and satisfying in the whole of gardening. From there she went on to propagate for sale and gradually, by dint of lecturing, showing (her Gold Medal exhibits at Chelsea became world-famous, and in 1988 the Royal Horticultural Society conferred on her its highest award for services to horticulture, the Victoria Medal of Honour), writing and building up a tremendous plantsman's nursery enterprise, she discovered a way forward. The responsibilities and strains have been great and, although matriarchal to all her staff, she has never been the

In the Gravel Garden, converted from a car-park, spires of *Kniphofia* 'Sunningdale Yellow' with *Brachyglottis* (*Senecio*) 'Sunshine' in the foreground.

best of delegators (she would not accept this),★ but she has been blessed with a strong constitution and she has always lived sensibly, preferring a vegetarian diet, although never imposing this on others, or insisting on it herself when away from home. All the same, worries don't go away, when so many people, including a husband who has for long been a sick man, depend on you. So many of the most admirable enterprises depend on the gifts of one person and her admirers must learn from them while they may.

In her gardening, Beth Chatto is exceptionally clear-sighted. She is very broad-minded and far more catholic in her tastes than many of her adulators realize. She is attracted to an amazing range of different kinds of plants, seeing how they can be used, often in unconventional ways, but so as to bring out the best in them. 'I detest cannas,' many people will say, if they even know what a canna is. In their minds they have a vision of the unimaginative treatment of cannas in public parks and gardens, used perhaps in summer bedding as dot plants. These people cannot sort out the intrinsic merits and possibilities of the plant. Beth can, and I would defy anyone seeing them in

★ And, on being shown the manuscript, she did not. I should explain that, with a staff of some twenty-five, she obviously delegates the details of running garden and nursery, but on the larger issues she remains the lonely pinnacle in a one-woman enterprise.

the little courtyard on to which her utility room looks out to say that they weren't just right the way she uses them, say with the boldly white-striped foliage of that splendid grass, *Arundo donax* 'Variegata', or with the blue-leaved rosettes of echeverias, with aeoniums, agaves and less stiff pelargoniums.

She can walk into a strange garden and instantly sum up what is good about it and what it lacks or what has somehow been done wrong. Questioned on this, by the owners, usually anxious to profit from the occasion, Beth can come out with a stream of excellent suggestions, such as will leave the owners quite breathless, yet full of gratitude, and rightly so.

She is always on the lookout for new plants, new to her, ones that are usually without much public recognition. She studies their habitat requirements and finds out how and where they grow in nature so that she can treat them appropriately – this is something she learned early on from her husband, who has made a lifelong study of ecology and of plant communities in the wild. If she sees a moisture- and shade-loving plant next to a basker that will be happy on the driest gravel, it worries her, even if both plants are flourishing. She feels it is wrong. I sometimes part company with her in that respect.

Having decided which plants she wants to grow and where, as also how to make them as happy as a plant can be, she is brilliant in her arrangement of them to make a three-dimensional picture that can, if necessary, be enjoyed from every direction. OK, she does use many soft colours and a great deal of grey, but she is not frightened of bright colours, as it might be *Crocosmia* 'Lucifer', either. She will set it among the fresh green inflorescences of self-sowing *Bupleurum falcatum*.

Cardoons and opium poppies in the new Gravel Garden.

I remarked, apropos of the widely held inhibitions which people hamper themselves with over colour combinations, that pink and yellow are not supposed to go well together (they could look awful, of course; it depends on the size and brilliance of the flowers and the setting they are in). 'I love pink and yellow,' said Beth, 'I'm constantly using it,' and the example in front of us had the Spanish broom, *Spartium junceum*, next to a bright pinky-mauve tree mallow, *Lavatera* 'Bredon Springs'. But hard by them were cardoons, with their big, jagged grey leaves, and a deep pink opium poppy, whose bold, glaucous foliage is so important.

Beth has always placed the importance of foliage above that of flowers. It is with you for so much longer, and for sheer size, leaves are often far more impressive than flowers can match up to.

White Barn House is the single-storey, though split-level, home purpose-built for the Chatto family around 1960 in a part of the farm that was considered impossible for cultivation. It is five miles east of Colchester, in Essex, on the road to the seaside resort of Clacton. Essex is our second largest county but mainly flat and featureless and with a low rainfall of around 20 inches (500 mm) per annum. It is bleak, too, being largely unprotected from easterly winds off the Continent, in winter.

The site of what was to become the garden was entirely overgrown with scrub – blackthorn, willow and brambles, though with a few good oaks; gravel on the slopes, ill-drained clay at the bottom. But there was a quite definite slope on the ground – a blessing in these parts – which was made into two terraces below the house and allowed an overview. And there was a spring-fed, year-round stream at the bottom. Who wouldn't be glad of that, in lowland Britain?

Beth never does anything by halves. She always takes immense trouble in preparing the ground before ever a plant goes in; by draining, where necessary, deep cultivation and the incorporation of immense quantities of organic matter. In her early book *The Dry Garden*, you can follow how she converted an arid, gravelly area where virtually nothing would grow in summer into a garden redolent of the south of France, using drought-tolerant plants, though many others would also have flourished.

This area, the first to be developed, is known as the Mediterranean garden. It lies on a south-west-facing slope and suits baskers. I never thought that heathers looked appropriate in it (though whether ecologically correct, I hardly know), but they seem to have gone and are not missed. Although Beth Chatto is renowned for specializing, on her nursery, in perennials, she appreciates the backbone value of shrubs and trees and is no less interested in them. So the hot spots have cistuses, sages and other aromatic shrubs of the maquis, brooms (an old, presiding Mount Etna broom, *Genista aetnensis*, which cascades at 15 feet with scented yellow blossom in July, has finally departed, but it is not a shrub you give up; you replace), spurges – forms of *Euphorbia wulfenii* look particularly compact and well furnished – and grey-leaved buddleias. Beds tend to be raised a little and to be tactfully edged with concrete, to prevent soil from spilling on to the paths.

There is a new raised bed in front of a wall, dividing nursery from garden, suitable for all sorts of small things and cushion-formers. My eye was taken by a grouping where a moss green raoulia mat was rubbing cheeks with the succulent *Sedum dasyphyllum*, then (in June) smothered with its flesh pink blossom but pierced here and there with tufts of *Sisyrinchium angustifolium*, with narrow gimlet leaves and blue stars that open at midday. Behind, a glaucous mound of roseroot, *Rhodiola rosea* (*Sedum roseum*). Its terminal, lime green inflorescences give it the casual appearance of a spurge. That had already flowered in May.

But before you come to this area you are close to the house, in whose vicinity Beth sets out a community of pots for summer enjoyment. Some of them are changed around, being brought on to the scene when approaching their big moment and taken away afterwards. The Scarborough lily, for instance, which carries umbels of soft, yet bright, red open funnels, in September. It is nothing much to look at before or after. You just want it for those few weeks. We knew it as *Vallota speciosa*, but are now told to call it *Cyrtanthus elatus*; some old habits die hard, however. Most of the pots will remain in position throughout the summer and autumn season. Ivy-leaved pelargoniums will twine affectionately around the stiff, prickle-edged leaves of variegated *Agave americana*. I liked the juxtaposition, one year (these things change quickly), of fleshy aeonium rosettes with columns of deep blue-green *Euphorbia wulfenii* foliage, the latter growing in the ground at the end of the house. Last time I was there, this position was dominated by the aforementioned grass, *Arundo donax* 'Variegata', next to a handsome red pelargonium, the two of them set off by the purple foliage of a vine against the house, *Vitis vinifera* 'Purpurea'.

It is important to have something nice to look out on from a working sink, and Beth's utility room window, after seeing through a planting close against it (I mentioned the red canna/variegated grass combination), takes the eye to an inviting seat on the courtyard's other side and the bold-leaved *Vitis coignetiae* encircling it and clothing the wall behind. To the left, a handsome pile of sawn firewood is stacked beneath an awning, but there is space beside this for pots of the sky blue annual convolvulus, *Ipomoea tricolor*, well called morning glory. Such a thrill when a new crop of its magical trumpets opens at each

Pond reflections with arum lilies (*Zantedeschia aethiopica*) in the foreground.

break of day. In a fairly central position within this courtyard is a raised oblong sink, filled with house leek (*sempervivum*) rosettes. This is a private area and needs to be. The public is hopelessly light-fingered when tempted by rosettes of this kind.

The sitting/eating-out terrace, on the other side of the utility/bedroom wing, looks down on a cool and inviting prospect, with a chain of ponds and a mature oak behind them as your main focal points, though trees that Beth planted – weeping willow, swamp cypress (*Taxodium*) and the similarly deciduous though faster-growing *Metasequoia* – are already well developed. Another deciduous conifer that I love and which is growing enviably well here, you pass on your left as you take the direct route down steps to the ponds. This is *Pseudolarix amabilis*, a larch-like tree, though less vigorous and of more spreading habit, its cones like miniature globe artichokes. Its foliage in summer is of the freshest green, changing to pure lemon yellow before falling.

Of the older garden areas, I like the pond plantings best. They have a sumptuous lushness that feels cool and luxuriant even in the heat of the day, for there is full exposure to sunlight, which is what best suits waterside plants, so long as the moisture is there.

There are three or four ponds in a chain, divided by dams across which you walk. Bold leaves predominate, particularly those of *Gunnera tinctoria*, which are like those of *G. manicata* and just as large, when well grown, but more crimped, making a frillier impression. The water saxifrage, *Darmera peltata*, seems like a mini-version of this, though it also carries umbels of pink flowers on rhubarb pink stems, in April, before a leaf is in sight. That, too, is the way of the giant yellow arum, *Lysichitum americanum*, dramatic in early spring with its clusters of bright yellow spathes, but contributing handsomely, later on, with bouquets of broadly lanceolate, dark green, shiny leaves.

The florists' arum lilies, with spathes of purest white focused by a yellow spadix club at the centre, love rich soil at a pond's margin, whether in a few inches of water or just above it on the bank. Their hardiness is always being questioned, but I have never seen them looking more at home than here, where they seem totally in their element, reflected in the water (and never forget that their bold arrow leaves are a necessary contribution to the picture). I admit that they also look fine within a box-hedged cabin in the white garden at Sissinghurst Castle, but in their element? No.

Another leaf I enjoy, floating raft-like over the surface of these ponds, is the bog bean's, *Menyanthes trifoliata*. It is indeed rather bean-like, trifoliate and pointing over the pond with confidence. It flowers charmingly in early May, with loose spikes of frilly-edged white stars, pink in the bud.

Strap leaves are the perfect foil to those of rounded shape, so there are various water-loving irises and tall grasses, notably the 10-foot *Miscanthus floridulus*, with a fountain-like habit, and a zebra grass, *M. sinensis* 'Zebrinus', in which the leaves are cross-banded, at intervals, with greeny yellow blotches. In late summer and autumn, these are joined by the tall domed mauve platforms of *Eupatorium purpureum* and its more intensely purple variant, 'Atropurpureum' (now considered to be a variety of *E. maculatum*).

There is a broad, shady walk behind these ponds, with masses of *Cyclamen hederifolium* flowering in autumn beneath the oak. Ferns set them off. Beth is as fond of ferns as you would expect. In a steepish, shady border at the lower end of the ponds, there is a wonderful foliar combination, each plant in totally contrasted shape and colouring: a finely dissected lady fern, *Athyrium filix-femina*, clumped at the back; then a swathe, following the contour, of a dwarf grass, *Hakonechloa macra* 'Aureola', which is more yellow than green; in front, a broad, waxy blue-leaved hosta. Not far off, two more, clumpy, ferns, *Polystichum setiferum* 'Acutilobum', with quite muscular, evergreen fronds; *Cystoperis bulbifera*, delicate and deciduous; but interweaving between them, a ground-hugging ivy, with pale creamy leaf margins.

At the lowest, boggy level, there is a border gay with flowers in early summer: white foxgloves, bright candelabra primulas, the sweetly scented and most old-fashioned day lily, *Hemerocallis flava* (now *H. lilio-asphodelus*), yellow mimulus, a haze of blue water forget-me-not, *Myosotis scorpioides*. Then, as you approach (camera at the ready, needless to say), your eye focuses and it is a fern again, the hart's-tongue, with the elegant side shoots of a white foxglove hanging over it. 'A simple little statement,' was Beth's comment when I pointed this out to her. Such is the jargon of the garden.

You reach the reservoir garden, which I think of as fairly new, though it dates back over fifteen years now. Following the disastrous drought of 1976, the neighbouring fruit grower needed to enlarge the reservoir which takes the overflow from the stream feeding the Chattos' ponds. The clay from this was spread over the gravel bank above it, and Beth made all this palatable to plants by top-dressing heavily and continuously with spent compost from the nursery, mainly peat and sand, with farmyard manure and dressings of straw. Straw is an ugly mulch, so she keeps it in the background or middle of beds beneath trees and shrubs, preferring to cover the wide border margins with crushed bark.

I should, perhaps, digress a moment, to say that on principle there is no irrigation in the garden, only in the nursery, where it is absolutely necessary for the existence of the business. Beth feels that much water is extravagantly and needlessly wasted in an area where supplies are often short, and she deliberately sets an example by her use of mulches, of which bark is the favourite. It keeps annual weeds at bay (the perennials can be given individual treatment by painting them with herbicide) and it keeps the soil beneath cool and moist. Sometimes I find it a little obtrusive and refer to the Beth Chatto Bark Garden, which deserves a spanking, I know. It saves a great deal of expensive labour, in the long run, and that well compensates for the initial outlay.

The borders of which the reservoir garden is composed are so large that they form their own backgrounds and you would never think of them as island beds – those squirming horrors that students in horticultural colleges are taught to admire. The borders are divided by broad grass paths. All look thoroughly mature now, as where the pink cranesbill 'Claridge Druce', with its questing habit, weaves into the lowest branches of the Serbian spruce, *Picea omorika*. One extremely bold and successful planting has the giant umbels of angelica as background to the 6-foot spires of *Delphinium* 'Alice Artindale', which has double blue flowers and is the very best for drying, as it keeps its shape so well.

Beth Chatto is always seeking new outlets for her creativity, though she does appreciate the danger of established features, which are repeatedly in

need of renewal, being neglected in favour of the latest enterprise. Beyond the reservoir garden we are in a piece of woodland, which has now been turned into another feature, a woodland garden. As usual, infinite trouble has been taken in the preparation and excavation of the ground, incorporating the best possible soil, compost and mulches. The plants are loving it. How often, for instance, do you see colonies of arisaemas in south-east England? I was just on cue for *Arisaema tortuosum*, a tall and slender aroid with a green and white spathe from which protrudes a twisting, green, tail-like spadix.

A contrast in colour and form: the double *Delphinium* 'Alice Artindale' against *Angelica archangelica*.

At the far side of this woodland, which Beth still keeps private, as it is below her nursery stock beds which are themselves not public territory, there is another ditch on her property's boundary, and that has a year-round spring feeding it, so another area for shade- and moisture-loving plants is being made alongside.

But her biggest innovation to date has been the new gravel garden, on the site of the old car-park, which was much too close to her house for comfort. She was able to buy a piece of neighbouring land (more unprofitable fruit) and to move the car-park out towards the new boundary. Where it had been, the ground was horribly compacted. Once more the deepest excavations and cultivations were made, and soil improvements. Areas for planting were outlined – it would be wrong to call them anything so formal as beds, since the plantings merge into the gravel and the gravel runs right through the plantings. But all the plants were in position before this fine gravel was introduced. Besides acting as a theme it is also a mulch.

I saw the gravel garden only fourteen months after it had been planted, and it looked wonderfully established. It would have been hard to guess that it was actually so new, though the shrubs in it will, of course, assume considerably greater bulk. At times, in the run up, Beth felt daunted at the prospect of all the placing and planting on which she would need to concentrate in a life that was already one long series of engagements and interruptions. She saw it through and I feel that this has been the crowning achievement of all the experience and artistry of a lifetime. This kind of art is ephemeral; we have to savour it on the spot and at its moment, but it is no less important or vitalizing than any other (albeit more enduring) art form, be it painting, music, ceramics or architecture.

Gardening demands a feeling for shape and form and colour and a love and understanding for the plant itself, which is a living work of nature. To have or to make the opportunities for exploiting these talents requires a certain amount of good fortune, but to seize your chances as Beth Chatto has is the ultimate. I salute her with love and with admiration.

England: West and South-West

MAPPERTON HOUSE

—⟶◦⟵—

I FIRST VISITED Mapperton House on a perfect May Day morning, not a cloud in the sky, not a soul in the garden, the countryside fresh and vernal. I was staying with Anna Pavord in her Dorset home a few miles distant. She and Fergus Garrett were my companions, in the absence but with the permission of Caroline and John Montagu, the owners. I had no idea what to expect.

Mapperton was a manor mentioned in Domesday, and the manorial buildings make a delightful group as you approach, most of the buildings dating from the sixteenth and seventeenth centuries, though partly reworked in the eighteenth. All are built of local Ham Hill stone. So you have the house on your left, a stable block courtyard on your right, the church and a dovecote just beyond the house. At this season, progress is delayed by the sight and scent of wisteria blossom on the south face of the north stable building.

The public's entrance to the gardens is actually better than from the house itself. It takes you on to a very large, flat, rectangular area of lawn, the north (and oldest) wing of the house forming its southern boundary on your right, walls (not interestingly planted) on the lawn's west and north sides, nothing but an open view of the countryside beyond, to the east. You walk, a trifle grumpily, towards this open side. 'A massive area of grass,' was Fergus's comment, and I still think that I should want to break it, say with a group of small trees like *Cornus kousa*, *Amelanchier* or *Crataegus*.

As you approach the lawn's far margin, you realize that something peculiar is happening. Anna kept quiet, all this while; she wasn't going to spoil the revelation. Before you know quite what has happened, there, in front of and below you, is a magical Italianate formally constructed garden, overlaid with the softness bestowed by time and the borrowed landscape, behind, of intimate Dorset slopes, trees, a post and rail boundary fence and cows beyond.

You are looking down steeply sloping grass terraces into a narrow little valley, nowhere more than 50 yards across, and in this the garden has been laid

Looking back to Mapperton House across the Fountain Court, before the raised pool area was restored.

out. We sat down on the lip of the first grassy terrace and for a considerable while (time is suspended, on these precious occasions) just soaked it all in.

Gardens like this don't just happen; they have a considerable past, something of which we gradually learned. The family which by linear and collateral descent had owned Mapperton for centuries sold it to Mr and Mrs Labouchère in 1919, and she it was, during the course of a very long life, who created most of the main features of the garden as we see it. There is much terracing, mostly in local stone, though the eastern wall is brick; paving, steps, seats and statuary, all in charming proportions and supported by topiary in yew and box.

In a series of important, stepped pieces (shaped like a cash register with the drawer open), which themselves flank and make a lead up actual steps (of composite stone), yew overlays box plinths. These, as is the way of topiary

An exciting prospect is revealed as you reach the far side of the big lawn on the upper level.

and hedging, have become somewhat bulbous and overgrown. Yew can be rejuvenated. It responds well to being cut hard back into its centre. Box, less well or predictably in the outcome. Therein lies a problem.

John Montagu's father, Victor, bought the property in 1955. He was an avid and restless gardener. All his purchases and their siting are meticulously recorded in large files, whom they were bought from, whether they died and, if so, with what they were replaced. He also made alterations and additions to the garden's structure.

The area we were looking down on, as we sat on the turf, is called the Fountain Court. A number of springs and small watercourses flow into the valley and feed its ponds. They also worked the small fountains that gave this garden its name, but these features need a good deal of upkeep. The water table sometimes falls so that they could not work anyway.

This is the one chapter in *Other People's Gardens* that will identify only a few plants, since plants are subservient to structure. The Fountain Court has a raised pool, shaped rather like a tortoise, in its centre, which has recently been relined with concrete. The rather puny beds that surrounded it have been eliminated and gravelled over. I did slightly miss the stonecrops (sedums) that were colonized around its supporting feet, but they are fast returning. Crazy paving on the floor of this garden is in local stone, though varied, in one strip, with a herringbone pattern in brick. I do like that sort of touch.

This garden's main axis runs north–south, dropping southwards with the line of the valley. But there is a shorter east–west axis, with shallow steps rising

The Garden House seen above a canal, turned swimming-pool.

in each direction to a summerhouse built into the side of the valley and a fireplace in each. I wonder how often that was used!

Mrs Labouchère was active at a time when reconstituted stone, a mixture of ground stone and cement, was just becoming widely used and there is much of it here – in the steps, in some of the seats and in some of the statuary. Statuary is prolific, though never overdone, except from the point of view of upkeep. There are many stone or 'stone' animals and birds (six cranes), some in a sad state of decomposition, but decay has its own charm, if you are not yourself responsible for arresting it. The bold leaves of bergenias make a good foreground to masonry, and you notice them here.

There is a wide pergola with four lines of reconstituted stone pillars linked by wooden cross beams. This used to be in two sections, the upper one close to, though not centred upon, a large greenhouse at the top, north, end of this garden. Victor Montagu's principal work, in 1968, was to replace the greenhouse with an orangery to terminate the vista on the garden's main axis. To make the intention more prominent, he removed the top section of the pergola and transplanted it to the Fountain Court's lower end, where it now forms a continuation to its other half.

Unsupported by any plantings, the orangery, although in the right place for such a feature, is aggressively dominant; it doesn't tie into the hillside. Measures are now being taken to mitigate this (short of moving the half-pergola back again) with finials of two upright Irish yews in front, another pair of 'cash register' topiary features and a clothing of wall shrubs and creepers on the building itself. Some hardwood trees – beech, oak and ash – have been planted behind it and will make a backdrop.

At the lower end of the Fountain Court and plumb centre in the axial line rises a tall, narrow Garden House. It has an upstairs room (with a fireplace) and a view down on to two ponds, with woodland and fields beyond, still with the feel of a small, intimate yet detailed landscape, abundant in contours. This Garden House seems to include fairly ancient elements but they have been muddied by extensive alterations in Victorian times.

The temptation is now to turn aside, eastwards, and to explore a more intimate, indeed overcrowded area (until recently thinned and restored to order by Kirsty Fergusson, who spent several years gardening here) having nothing to do with the formal garden. There is a little fountain basin fed from a natural spring and bubbling beneath four steps to emerge again below them and continue on its way to the pools. There are cyclamen, for autumn, and primroses for spring. Cyclamen also thrive beneath an enormous weeping beech and this has polypody ferns growing on its buttresses. There are bluebells, too. The shrubbery, planted by Colonel Daniel, a friend of the

The canals melt into the Wild Garden and then the Dorset countryside. To the left, a beautiful group of Scots pines, *Pinus sylvestris*.

family, is called Daniel's Garden. But its crowning glory preceded him: a group of mature Scots pines. Their roseate trunks glow in low sunshine, particularly towards evening, and can be admired from most parts of the garden, as also from the house.

You will probably return to the garden's main axis between the upper and lower pools, both long, canal-like rectangles, flanked on each side by a row of trimmed yews. The upper pool, converted to a swimming-pool, leads the eye back to the Garden House, whose full height can be appreciated from here. It is an endearing feature. Nothing at Mapperton is daunting, although it is difficult to write of architectural features without their seeming so. A lovely patina of mosses and lichens, everywhere. Dorset has a pretty high rainfall.

Looking downhill, the lower pool has a grand planting of yuccas (dating back to Mrs Labouchère's day) at the far end. What an excellent placing for a determined and terminating feature. I should love to see them in flower. Most were budding up freely when I was there on my second visit, in mid-July.

It is worth exploring below this pool, where Victor Montagu created something of an arboretum, called the Wild Garden. There is a tunnel of bamboos with bright green canes, and interesting trees. These included a mature *Malus hupehensis*, whose trunk develops large, scaly plates. The blossom, pink in bud, opens to pure white with large individual blooms. Another crab, *M. crataegifolia* (now *M. florentina*), has indented leaf margins more like a hawthorn's or an oak's, grey-green in youth. Masses of bud promised a good display shortly. At its lower end, the Wild Garden merges into woodland. Meantime, the stream bed at the valley bottom has been partially planted along its steepish margins with gunneras and willows. There would be great scope for a thoroughgoing water garden feature.

But you don't want too busy a gardener at Mapperton. They might plant a huge rose garden, where roses didn't want to be, or they might make yet another white garden. The spirit of the place doesn't suit that sort of business. Lots of self-sowing cotoneasters in decayed walls and paving is much more in its style, and they are plentiful. They would have to be removed as repairs were made but would find a home somewhere.

As a keen gardener, one of my chief concerns and frustrations would be the damage done by vagrant deer. There is a herd of fallow deer in the locality, of which the locals (those who don't suffer from them) are proud, and roe deer, also. Anything is liable to be eaten, up to deer height. Deer fencing would be extremely expensive and probably unacceptably ugly, though I don't believe that has to be the case. Deer have a particular taste for roses, incidentally. Human or, better still, lion's hair suspended about the place in bags is said to be a deterrent. You could make a new sort of garden.

Mapperton gardens are open a good deal of the time. Five thousand visitors was the sort of gate expected when I was there. That's not nearly enough. It's only a slightly out-of-the-way spot, but as Anna remarked, 'Joe Bloggs in the street doesn't need to go to Mapperton because it hasn't got enough ice cream.'

English Heritage have published an excellent report, written by Georgina Livingston, on the gardens and are supporting them from their storm damage fund, following the January 1990 storm. Their interpretation of this is fairly liberal. Along the lip of the North Lawn, from where the visitor gets his first view of the formal gardens below, a yew hedge has recently been planted.

There was a beech hedge here, which Mrs Labouchère removed. When the hedge has grown, the view will be revealed not gradually but startlingly, as you reach one of the gaps in this hedge. We like what we are used to. The pros and cons for this hedge could be argued either way.

English Heritage have supported other plantings, notably of trees in the landscape. To my eye, this didn't look undesirably denuded. There seemed to be trees enough, but one has to look ahead. Many have been lost, either to elm disease or by storm destruction or from old age (which a storm is liable to catch out). Youngsters coming along are certainly a good plan.

Many walls and much masonry needs rebuilding. It remains to be seen what can be afforded. English Heritage provide only a percentage of costs. Much would be left in the lap of the Montagu family. One wishes them well from the bottom of one's heart. And one wishes that they may enjoy Mapperton as an ongoing love affair transcending the cares and responsibilities that are always attendant upon property.

CHILCOMBE

———◆◆◆———

CHILCOMBE was one of the gardens that I visited with Fergus Garrett from Anna Pavord's, while staying with her in Dorset (see also Kingston Maurward, Mapperton House, Stourton House and Overbecks). The first time was in May, the second in July the following year. This is the home of John and Caryl Hubbard, and it is only just across the valley from the Old Rectory at Puncknowle, where Anna lives. Both are close to the Channel and chilling sea fogs drift in with disconcerting frequency, even at the height of summer. But the hilly Dorset countryside – Hardy's Wessex – is wonderful; surprisingly unspoilt and with the feeling of being far from London, though this is about as close to London as you can get this feeling. Buzzards hang on the air. Some people have all the luck. Why can't I have buzzards at Dixter? I would have a bird feeder made specially and furnish it with delicious rabbits, ready to kill.

The Hubbards have two terriers and they are to Chilcombe very much as my two dachshunds are to Dixter – a fundamental part of the place. On their front door, they have the simple notice, *Chien Gentil*, which my animals could never aspire to. It isn't strictly true of theirs, which are fine with grown-ups but detest children, as one child was not slow to point out. Of course, there are exceptional children but by and large, can you blame the dogs?

It was on a bright Sunday morning, when the virtuous (Caryl Hubbard and Celly Clark) were just about to attend matins in the adjoining church, that the less virtuous John, Fergus and myself started on our detailed garden tour. John had been 'up a ladder with a mouthful of string', with which he was tying roses.

John Hubbard is a well-known artist and this is invariably referred to as an artist's garden. It is that. Obviously, if you are an artist and also a gardener, your garden becomes an artist's garden. However, more significance than that is put into the straightforward fact. John sees his garden through an artist's eyes. Ah! How must that feel? we non-artists reverentially wonder.

A relaxed area at the bottom of the garden with mixed plantings in rectangular beds, enclosed by cement brick paths. The showy *Potentilla × hopwoodiana* is prominent in the foreground.

Clearly he cannot be seeing the world as we are (neither does anyone else, come to that; we are all individuals with our own individual perceptions). John plays up to the role assigned him very well. As a complete *non sequitur*, I should mention that he is, or was, American but has for so long been domiciled in Britain that you would scarcely know it even from any lingering brogue.

We stood for at least half an hour in the front courtyard. It has magic. It was the yard between the kitchen and servants' quarters (the fifteenth-century doorway of which now comprises the entrance to the later building) and the old manor house, removed in 1938. The surviving house, to which the Hubbards moved in 1969, was built around the turn of the seventeenth and eighteenth centuries. The windows are mullioned, not sash, as they became in Georgian times.

This yard is paved with stone, but was inches deep in soil when first the Hubbards arrived. Now it is full (but not overfull) of mat-forming and self-seeding plants in the cracks. There are wild strawberries, restrained from sending their runners over all the paving; *Alchemilla mollis*, cut back when it starts to look tatty and largely prevented from seeding; lamb's lugs, *Stachys lanata*, and the smaller-leaved but even paler grey *Cerastium tomentosum*, called snow-in-summer – 'Such a nice name,' said John. The slender yet spiky toadflax, *Linaria purpurea*, has upward thrust; there is woodruff, Welsh poppy, bloody cranesbill, forget-me-nots. A few shrubs, too: *Salvia microphylla neurepia*, whose deep, warm pink flowers are borne all through summer and autumn; variegated dogwood, *Cornus alba*; a buddleia; soft pink *Lavatera* 'Barnsley'; *Hydrangea villosa*.

A good team, but besides these there are pots standing around that impose a greater sense of order. They also allow more tender plants to be grown, like *Helichrysum petiolare*, *Verbena* 'Sissinghurst', the climbing *Sollya fusiformis*, with little lanterns in pure blue; the splendid bromeliad-like *Eryngium pandanifolium*; but even more dominant than this, surprisingly, a fine clump of a good form of *Salvia guaranitica*, of upstanding habit, with bold, glossy leaves and terminal racemes of deep blue flowers.

Wherever you stand, whichever way you turn, you see or glimpse something else. Domestic offices are contained in a low building added by the Hubbards and covered with a luxuriance of *Parthenocissus henryana*. What better Virginia creeper than that? It grows in a relaxed way, and its fingered leaves are neat and beautifully marked and generally change to wonderful warm colours in autumn (mine doesn't). In the opposite direction there is a genuine Gothic doorway through the old wall, and through it you catch inviting glimpses – of arum lilies in May or of peachy alstroemerias in July.

A Hubbard terrier, bathing. *Zantedeschia aethiopica*, the florist's arum lily, flourishes outside, here.

The garden is not large but is divided into many little compartments. You are delayed by your immediate surroundings, yet aware that there is much going on and to be seen beyond them.

The arum lilies flank a ground-level basin, into which water drops musically but without haste. The terriers love to wallow in it. The water is supplied from a spring up the hill and there is another supply, also their own, for the garden, so they are not dependent on the water board's whims.

This water feature, together with table and chairs, is at the end of an extensive lawn – the only one at Chilcombe – which is level and flanks the house's garden front. The garden door into the house is invitingly led into by steps, having simple, curved, white-painted iron railings either side of them. Flanking these, there are bushes of *Ceanothus* 'Henri Desfosse', with deep indigo panicles. It is the weakest-growing of its group, which also includes 'Gloire de Versailles' and 'Topaz', but was growing quite strongly.

Here, also in the border opposite and in a number of other places, grew the stately clary, *Salvia sclarea* 'Turkestanica'. It is biennial, so you never know quite where to expect it next and it self-sows happily on light or chalky soils; here they are on greensand. This sage grows stiffly to about 4 feet and opens a candelabrum of mauve flowers and bracts over a long period. Definitely a plant with a presence.

The 4-foot-wide border on the far side of the lawn from the house is in front of a 4-foot-high wall, over which you get a sighting of the next bit of garden, but also, more importantly, of the countryside beyond. It is lovely to feel enclosed, but no less exhilarating to see out and to be aware of a wonderful world beyond.

The border at your feet includes another sage, *Salvia verticillata*, much more compact than I have seen it in the wild and with richer purple flowers. There are also a number of penstemons. John and Caryl are fond of *Penstemon heterophyllus* 'Heavenly Blue' and of the rather similar *P. glaber*, which is lilac-coloured, stays low and flowers twice if the first crop is dead-headed. I wouldn't give space to either, myself. The pale mauve form of *Viola cornuta* is here, and bright little yellow stars from a sisyrinchium. This being the first yellow flower that I had noticed, I asked John how he felt about this colour. So many gardeners of good taste dislike it. 'We used to be anti; now we're very pro,' he said. But he hates the double yellow Banksian rose; so does Anna Pavord. I wonder why. It seems innocuous to me.

From the garden below, the pink rose 'Fantin Latour' and the mauve potato flower, *Solanum crispum*, top the wall by 18 inches or so. Nice to be greeted by next door, like that.

The entrance to the walled garden has an unruly (though carefully pruned) *Buddleia alternifolia* making an arch over it. Its long wands of mauve blossom, clothing the last year's new shoots along most of their length, can look great during their June flowering, but there is nothing to follow and the shrub has little personality at other seasons. Fergus, the third party, describes what followed. 'A large *Buddleia alternifolia* hanging over a hole in the wall. Christo, not impressed, tried to convince John that he could do better. John states, "I like its mad shape, and I like walking under it." Christo, not having any of this nonsense, states a practical fact: "When it's raining and you walk through it, you get wet." John: "Yes, you get wet" (not convinced; Christo loses).'

Well, so you're down into the walled garden. If you turn to the right, there are espalier apples on your left underplanted with a ribbon of self-heal in its domesticated (this being otherwise a weed, especially in lawns) pink form, 'Loveliness'. At the end of these espaliers, an 'Étoile Violette' clematis has been allowed to interlope and it also mingles with 'Blush Noisette', a charming rose with blush pink clusters. Here, also, is the thornless rambler 'Bleu Magenta'. Throw in the mauve-flowered rambler 'Veilchenblau' (violet blue), spread over the studio at the bottom of the garden, and you have a fair idea of the colours that are 'very John Hubbard', as Fergus put it. These roses are subject to mildew (as to other rose ailments) but they are a major, though not dominant, theme at Chilcombe and are taken very seriously. That includes an ongoing spray programme throughout the growing season.

'Étoile Violette' and 'Blush Noisette' are on or in (according to which side of it you're on) a corner, and you turn left into a rose pergola, whose stripped bark, tanalized pine posts (this is the third lot since 1970) are set into concrete footings. If you followed this to its end, you'd come, at right angles, to a narrow alley (too narrow; these features seldom foresee or cater sufficiently for the lateral spread of hedge ingredients; the yew alley at Sissinghurst has given much trouble in this respect), comprised mainly of green and purple beech but, so that the contrast between these two colours shall not punch you too aggressively between the eyes, they are mitigated with beech plants that are definitely less than purple, with yew and with both golden and plain green holly.

However, you will almost certainly not follow the pergola to its end but will turn left again into a rectangular garden which I would never dare to call a riot of colour; Fergus's 'a jungle of flowers' suits it better. The plantings are varied and saved from cottage garden messiness first by the layout, which is geometrical, in four pairs of rectangular beds, second, by the pots and sculpture. The pots, highly glazed, totally frost-proof and of broad and comfortable proportions, are a wonderful pair by Rupert Spira, given to Caryl by the Contemporary Art Society at the end of her term as Chairman. Another by Spira, under the yew tree by the church, was a swap for one of John's paintings. Wouldn't it be great to be able to barter at that level? The sculpture, by Peter Randall-Page, who takes his motifs from organic plant forms, is made of Kilkenny limestone.

This was a vegetable garden, but the more mundane, though still important, vegetables are nowadays grown below the main garden. There are herbs, still, including a handsome group of tansy, its bright green, dissected leaves contrasting well with purple-leaved sage (obviously the tansy would be the winner in this contest). One hot bed at the top of the slope is devoted to cistuses. You see the 'Étoile Violette' clematis from its other side and as a background, here, to regal lilies, *Knautia macedonica*, which is a dark, reddish purple scabious, and, tumbling over from the pergola, the ultra-vigorous Hybrid Musk rambler rose 'Francis E. Lester', with trusses of single, blush white blossom. The annual poppies, deriving from cornfield *Papaver rhoeas*, are in the pastel shades selected out by another artist, Sir Cedric Morris. Opium poppies feature here, too.

At the lower end of this garden there is a good deal of shade from the giant white cherry 'Tai Haku', with single flowers set off by bronze young foliage. John has successfully curbed the spread of this wide-elbowed tree by judicious pruning, without its appearing in the least maimed. An excellent grouping, here, again includes the excellent clematis 'Étoile Violette', which has a mass of flowers on its young growth that are of only moderate size, purple but with the focus of a creamy white eye. *Geranium psilostemon*, hoisting itself into it, and a pale mauve border phlox called 'Amethyst' (though sometimes

The cardoon, *Cynara cardunculus*, seemed, in May, to have unusually sculptural foliage.

'Prospero') make up the triangle. The cranesbill is bright purple, almost magenta, and has been given an almost black eye. Earlier in the previous year I had been impressed by a strain of cardoon, *Cynara cardunculus*, before it ran up to flower. Its pale leaves, less dissected than usual, were overlaid by an almost metallic sheen. This is a joyful garden.

The remains of an old orchard, with a grass sward beneath, are close by, the more decrepit trees having climbing roses planted at their feet. The garden's boundary wall, here (it's not too high and is easily looked over), has a fairly narrow, shady border in front of it, seasonally planted to brilliant effect with the yellow spires, black stems and orbicular leaves of *Ligularia* 'The Rocket' alternating, at its lower level, with greeny white astrantias and white shasta daisies, which follow a little later. To be really exciting like this, you need to limit your ambitions to a very few weeks in the year, though it would be perfectly feasible in this case to attain an equally charming winter/spring effect with such self-sowing colonizers as winter aconites, crocuses, primroses, perhaps some clumps of hepaticas. On the opposite side of the orchard lawn, a partially shaded border has tall clumps of pale mauve *Campanula lactiflora* and red nasturtiums in front. The idea is excellent, but nasturtiums are singularly unpredictable in their behaviour, often sulking just when you want them to be looking their brightest, or else hiding themselves beneath lush foliage. The garden, I may say, is all well fed with farmyard manure, their own compost and mushroom compost.

From here you step into the woodland walk. 'It's the thing we love more than anything else in the garden,' says John. 'That *you* love most,' corrects

The yellow spires of *Ligularia* 'The Rocket' contrasting with astrantias in a narrow border on the garden's boundary.

Caryl, who has rejoined us after church. It is twelve paces across if you don't step out too hurriedly. The cream panicles and pinnate leaves of *Sorbaria tomentosa* (*S. aitchinsonii*), a vigorous shrub that responds well to hard annual pruning, is the principal July feature. The orchard and woodland are restful before you emerge into another area of detailed planting. You might call it a potager – Caryl has rows of nine different kinds of basil, here – but everything is mixed in, to lively effect. Rectangular beds of cement bricks (*Salvia pratensis* seeds into the cracks) are edged by serpentine roof tiles, set vertically. Eight standard gooseberry bushes make a pleasing feature. They look so much more sensible than standard roses, besides making picking easy.

Very varied plantings, here. *Argyranthemum* 'Rollison's Red' made a good solid lump with sprays of 'Garnet' and 'Apple Blossom' penstemons rising behind it. Fergus noticed that bolted lettuces were looking nice with an osteospermum. They have a compact form of the mauve species *Dahlia merckii*; a mere 3 feet, compared with its more normal 7 feet. Besides the pink *Potentilla* 'Miss Willmott', which is a form of *P. nepalensis*, there was a showy and nearly related one called *P. × hopwoodiana*, having lights and shades in a salmon-coloured flower. A lot of the white (blush white, really) self-seeding mallow, *Malva moschata* 'Alba', which mixes well with the salmony pink racemes of *Diascia rigescens*. Nothing contrived, here; everything apparently thrown in together, wholly unpretentious yet basically organized. Gardens that appear to have done it themselves are often the ones on which most care has been lavished.

As you walk back up the slope (which has an easterly aspect), a highish boundary wall on your right has *Lonicera caprifolium* against it. This is one of the earliest-flowering honeysuckles, already in full bloom in early May, soft pink ageing buff and well-scented at night. 'A thing you wouldn't like that Alan (a mutual friend) gave me is the herbaceous elder.' 'I gave it to him,' was my comeback. It is Danewort, *Sambucus ebulus*, invasive but excellent in the right place, where it can be allowed to form a colony like bracken. It covers itself with corymbs of white blossom in later summer.

I was intrigued by the placing of a colony of *Crambe cordifolia*, where it stood out on a prominent corner. Seven feet tall, no wonder it looked important, though not yet, in early May, covered with its cloud of white blossom. Anna observed how its stems zig-zag as they go up, being apparently pushed outwards at each node by the leaf and its subtended spray of flowers.

There is a steep bank of thyme hereabouts. I wonder if the idea came from Sissinghurst. It does take a lot of weeding, dog violets being the principal invaders in this case.

On the July morning that I have been chiefly writing of, it was past 1.00 p.m. by the time we reached here and we had to hurry to the conservatory for a drink of Gewürztraminer before returning to our hostess at the Old Rectory. It is a really used conservatory, for sitting in and enjoyment. On my first visit, it was displaying a large specimen (they always are large) of the splendid shrubby cranesbill, *Geranium maderense*, full of its magenta blossom.

There is a feeling of great warmth at Chilcombe, but of an informing intelligence, also. Caryl and John Hubbard have strong ideas which they have worked out admirably over the years.

Lonicera caprifolium, a charming early-flowering species, fragrant at night.

STOURTON HOUSE

PURSUANT of our gardens visiting trip, Fergus Garrett and I, on 22 July, headed north from Anna Pavord's to Stourton House, picking up Edward Flint on the way. Edward was still a student at Wye College at the time and Fergus had graduated from there two years earlier. They were lively companions and Fergus took detailed notes, to which I am indebted for some of what follows.

It was a hot summer's morning and the whole countryside, or at least every front garden in it, was bursting with 'American Pillar' roses. Admittedly it is a shocking shade of shocking pink, and yet its ebullience disarms. As we drove through one village, suddenly there was an amazing burst of colour from an immaculately kept garden that had me squawking 'STOP'. Fergus reversed and we invaded it. Fergus headed for the front door and rang the bell, while I (more experienced) went round to the back and met the owners, Mr and Mrs Shelley, at once.

They were welcoming and it turned out (almost inevitable in the gardening world) that we had mutual friends. The lawn was perfect and in it was cut out a rectangular bed for large, double, tuberous begonias in clean, shining colours and another of Hybrid Tea roses. There was a rock garden and a mixed bed of shrubs and perennials, while Mr Shelley's vegetable and soft fruit garden, at the back, was as excellent in its way. It is a great pleasure to happen unexpectedly on a garden where much love, energy and commitment have so effectively been lavished.

This, I'm afraid, made us a half-hour late for our appointment at Stourton House, home of Colonel (Anthony) and Mrs (Elizabeth) Bullivant. (I regretfully record that the Colonel died a couple of years after our visit.) I first knew of Mrs Bullivant through an exhibit of dried flowers that she brought to one of the Royal Horticultural Society's winter shows in Westminster. It was set out at ground level, almost like a garden, and was entirely lacking in the stiff artificiality of dried flower arrangements as we have too often seen them

(though the quality of this art is becoming much more relaxed). She has subsequently given me a copy of her book, *Dried Fresh Flowers* (Pelham Books), which seems eminently sensible and well expressed, to me.

Stourton House, near to Mere in Wiltshire, is next to the car-park serving the famous National Trust property of Stourhead. It couldn't be more different: warm, personal, sometimes verging on the chaotic, but entirely lovable. The Bullivants came here in 1957. There are two full-time gardeners, Hugh (senior) and Paul, with extra help at key periods. The garden is largely geared to the production of material for Elizabeth's dried flower (and fruit) business. I am told that you can hardly move, in the house, for the quantities of drying and dried flowers hanging up.

'I hope you will come and see our non-complicated garden,' said Elizabeth, and we were off. Regal lilies alternating with delphiniums and some rather hectically coloured Floribunda roses dominated the first alley, and the next was lined by twelve overbearing false cypresses (*Chamaecyparis lawsoniana* cultivar, perhaps 'Allumii'), six on each side (one has died; it happens to all of us) – known as the twelve apostles. Originally bought under the impression that they would grow to 4 feet, they have now attained 25 feet. A single pink rambler rose hung coyly across the alley. Behind were rows of flowers and

The Herbaceous Garden, formally enclosed by undulating Leyland cypress hedges. A pool in the centre surrounds a flattish basin on a pedestal. Elizabeth Bullivant and Edward Flint passing through.

seed-heads for drying in what was once the vegetable garden. Some were annual, some perennial.

Leeks, for instance, are perennial, if given the chance. Asked how he grew them, Tom, the ex-gardener, replied laconically, 'Put 'em in the ground.' Their globular heads are cut just as they are setting their seed. *Alchemilla mollis*, with its cool, lime green sprays, is used in every bouquet. The big yellow thistle heads of *Centaurea macrocephala* were there and the bright, mustard yellow corymbs of the yarrow, *Achillea filipendulina* 'Gold Plate', golden rod, globe thistle (*Echinops*) and cherry-in-the-lantern (*Physalis*) were other perennials noted, not to mention the persistent and invasive weed, coltsfoot (*Tussilago*), which could present a nasty problem.

Of annuals, larkspurs, in mixed colours, were 4–5 feet tall and unsupported, but if they fall sideways, it doesn't matter, as kinked stems have their place in arrangements. *Limonium suworowii*, with its branching pink, tail-like panicles (its popular name is 'Pink Pokers'), has been grown as a conservatory pot plant whenever I've seen it before, but was flourishing in a row, here. I should like to try that as a border plant, in a sheltered spot.

About the only formally designed feature at Stourton House is a large square garden framed in tall, Leyland cypress hedging and having a central urn surrounded by a beautifully planted pool. There are three entrances

A delighfully chaotic border with self-sowing, self-perpetuating contents: poppies, melancholy thistle, *Allium sphaerocephalum*, *Lychnis coronaria* among them.

through the hedge (the top of which is undulating) by ogival archways. This hedge, which they started clipping from infancy, to make it dense and firm, now needs only (I was greatly surprised) one annual trim. This, in November, and yet in July it was looking by no means shaggy. Although this is called the Herbaceous Garden, the Bullivants were too sensible to be purists; there are shrubs, even a sizeable gum tree.

Within each corner is a flower bed, then a circular grass path and, within that, four large quarter-circular beds, each embracing a seat which faces the central feature. You can choose which seat to take according to the light (and your mood). This makes you feel very much a part of the garden. Although some plants were dotted about in the beds, others were large enough or grouped so as to give a more solid feel: the magnificent mauve lacecap *Hydrangea aspera villosa*, for instance, large tree peonies and hemp agrimony, *Eupatorium cannabinum*, with domed heads of fuzzy mauve blossom.

The central urn (a little tricky to reach for planting) contains tulips and Siberian wallflowers in spring; diascias, pelargoniums and fuchsias in summer. Around its pedestal there is a peat bed in the very clear water, containing

Double borders with *Lilium regale* in its prime.

A satisfying combination of *Hydrangea serrata* 'Bluebird' and hostas 'Halcyon' and 'Sun Power': *Dahlia merckii* peeping through.

Bowles's golden sedge, *Carex elata* 'Aurea', and the hardy pitcher plant, *Sarracenia flava*, of translucent lime green colouring. On days when the garden was open to the public, the Colonel used to conduct regular feeding sessions of this insectivorous plant, additionally offering Garibaldi squashed fly biscuits to visitors with insectivorous leanings. Another entertainment that he laid on was with the mouse plant, *Arisarum proboscideum*, an aroid whose spathe is drawn out into a tail-like projection. Add a squeak while you twist it around and the likeness to a mouse is inescapable. 'People like to be shown these things,' the Colonel explained.

In the pond, and in the moist cracks of paving around it, were moisture-loving plants, some wild, like common yarrow (*Achillea millefolium*); some introduced, like *Iris kaempferi* and brown-flowered *Sisyrinchium* 'Quaint and Queer'; these, with their spear leaves, contrasting with the scalloped foliage of *Alchemilla mollis*. There was mimulus, bog bean (*Menyanthes trifoliata*) and a small-leaved pink and white variegated bush willow, *Salix integra* 'Hakuro-nishiki'. Altogether a happy community.

Outside this enclosed garden, on a shaded piece of dry walling, grew a fungus with tiny grey cup-shaped fructifications. The Bullivants notice and appreciate that sort of thing. 'Oh look! It's going to have a flower,' Elizabeth exclaimed of an arisaema, which is another aroid with strange, unusual green or purple striped flowers that last only a few days and certainly deserve to be excited about. Here, in spring, flowers a collection of split corona daffodils. Many people loathe them as an unacceptable aberration, but if judged simply for themselves and without prejudice, you can see that many of them are very beautiful.

From this part of the garden I got two good ideas for plants to grow together. First, a blue-headed, blue-stemmed sea holly, *Eryngium × zabelii* 'Jewel', together with the pale yellow daisies of *Anthemis tinctoria* 'E. C. Buxton' or 'Wargrave' and a pale pink, small-flowered rose, as it might be 'The Fairy'. Second, with the emphasis on foliage and in a moderately shady situation, *Hosta* 'Halcyon', quite small-leaved and intensely blue, *Hosta* 'Sunpower', lime green and large-leaved, and the airy lacecap *Hydrangea serrata* 'Bluebird'. The small mauve flowers of a dwarf form of *Dahlia merckii* were pushing cheekily through the large hosta leaves.

I rather enviously (it has died on me) noted a really healthy bush of *Berberis thunbergii* 'Golden Ring', with masses of new growth. The leaves are purple, developing a narrow, pale green marginal line as they mature. Autumn colour is good. 'That's a different dragonfly, Ant; one of the big bombers,' Mrs Bullivant sang out at this point. She has very blue eyes and a very direct gaze.

We came to a semi-wild area where the garden fades and phases out into wilderness, yet nearly all can be used for the drying of flowers or seed-heads – oats, charlock, honesty, mugwort (*Artemisia*), Japanese wineberry coping admirably with wild stuff, *Lilium pyrenaicum* with ground elder. There were opium poppies, hogweed, columbines, a cultivated variety of potentilla, meadowsweet. All created a charming though unusual atmosphere, teetering on the brink of chaos.

Where a beech had fallen, the hollow left by its stump, when removed, was turned into a pond and fed with rainwater from the house roof, channelled to this spot. The bole of the fallen trunk is covered with creeper and has been turned into an arbour by dint of excavating a sunken pathway beneath it (this was Paul's idea).

The 'moat' is an open ditch lined with butyl, which loses itself under a hard path that runs parallel to the ditch but leaves a moist area (as also on the other side) between the two. This is planted with a range of moisture-lovers in bright, contrasting colours that make a thoroughly cheerful, if uncoordinated, display. Asked about colour, 'I don't plant my things to match up, but I plant them where I think they will be happy, and they do it themselves,' Elizabeth declared. It is a tonic to see such uninhibited gardening.

So here we had a range of astilbes and filipendulas, arum lilies, yellow and orange mimulus, magenta candelabra primulas, hostas, irises, red *Lobelia cardinalis*, the purple pokers of *Primula viali* with red tips where the buds are yet unopened, the sensitive fern, *Onoclea sensibilis*, with its pleasantly running habit (quite a weed in its native East Coast states of America) . . . 'Oh Ant, do look! There's a *very* fascinating dragonfly. I don't think I've seen that before.' Then: 'There's a snake.' It was a baby grass snake and not much favoured by

Astilbes, filipendulas, arum lilies (*Zantedeschia*) and irises by the 'moat'.

my hosts, who said they scared the visitors (of whom there had been 200 on the previous day).

In a picking border in front of the greenhouse, there was a galaxy of colour from field poppies in various shades, mauve opium poppies, reddish purple *Allium sphaerocephalum*, magenta-flowered *Lychnis coronaria* against grey stems and leaves, grey *Stachys lanata*, red-purple melancholy thistle, *Cirsium heterophyllum*, which runs, yarrow, which also runs, verbascums, eryngiums, hollyhocks at the back and some raucous Floribunda roses. By and large, a satisfying and delightful mix, though how to manage and control it would be a worry to many, more precisely minded, gardeners.

We were now near to the house's garden front, to which access has been blocked so that the wide steps leading down from it are untrodden and full of purple thyme and white-flowered *Sedum album*. Hart's-tongue and hard shield ferns as well as *Iris japonica*, all shade-lovers, were perfectly happy in blazing sun in two beds flanking the lowest step.

Here followed a big expanse of lawn, leading to a ha-ha and, beyond that, a thistly meadow with a decrepit tree in the middle, covered with a white canopy of the 'Kiftsgate' *Rosa filipes*. Mown grass does not go all the way to the ha-ha but there is a 2-metre-wide strip of uncut grass full, in July, of yellow lady's bedstraw. That was a charming touch. Three large cast-iron urns are stationed here and effectively divide relative formality from informality.

Across the lawn is the woodland garden. From the outside you are chiefly aware of large old rhododendron bushes and a frieze of hydrangeas, somewhat jostled, in front. Hydrangeas are a principal theme at Stourton House, being greatly valued for drying. In her book, Elizabeth is at pains to describe exactly the right stage at which to cull them for this purpose. Half this garden – the half I have so far been describing – is on neutral or alkaline soil, which tends to produce pink or red hydrangea flowers (those that are not white), while the other half, mainly comprising the woodland, with its rhododendrons and azaleas and the bulk of the hydrangea collection, gives rise to blue or purple hydrangea flowers.

At an RHS autumn show, quite recently, Elizabeth brought up a vase of 'Hamburg' hydrangea heads. This is a large-flowered, bun-headed hortensia. In colour, according to the age of the inflorescence, whether it grew on acid or alkaline soil and whether in sun or in shade, the flowers ranged from green to purple and deep bricky red, through deep blue and deep pink. All the colours were intense, but they varied to this amazing degree. Truly the hydrangea is versatile, especially when you add to its variability the differences between a bun-shaped inflorescence or a conical, and a head packed with sterile florets or a flat-topped lacecap wherein the sterile florets are arranged in an outer ring, while the central disc consists entirely of tiny fertile flowers.

The hydrangeas were Colonel Bullivant's principal concern and each variety was labelled, together with a legend telling you something about it. I was taken by a hortensia called 'Frillibet', with deckle-edged florets. It is a sport from the white 'Mme Emile Mouillère', one of the longest-flowering and most rewarding of all hydrangeas. Fergus liked the lacecap 'Lanarth White', which, with its fresh, rather pale green leaves, is excellent when it likes you but I have never been able to please it. I keep trying.

From the big lawn, there is a tiny passageway through to a secret garden, made from the core of a huge old rhododendron, cut out and removed. It had died after the 1976 drought. It contains a seat for two and a small rock garden planted with dwarf conifers, a blue spruce, heathers, dwarf azaleas and Japanese maples – a nice idea, though I didn't care a lot for the plantings.

The woodland plantings would, of course, look their best in spring, but there was a large colony of orange *Alstroemeria aurea* (*aurantiaca*) catching shafts of sunlight through gaps in the tree canopy. That was so good. Often denigrated as a weed because of its invasive, suckering habit, this alstroemeria can be truly appreciated when sited where its habits are a positive advantage.

Back at the house (clothed, incidentally, with *Wisteria sinensis* – a wonderful sight and scent in May), there is, outside the door on the west front, a bird feeder and weeds beneath. One of the Colonel's notices reads: 'The weeds here are from the bird-seed. We leave them. Birds like the greenery.' There had been quite a crop of cannabis seedlings in the previous year.

Elizabeth very kindly offered us lunch, which we had outside, where the public partake of teas on open days. There is a magnificent, mature variegated sycamore overhanging this area. It retains its lively cream and green stripy colouring all through the summer.

When Elizabeth emerged from the house with a saucepan in one hand and a frying pan in the other, I asked (in all innocence) if this was food for the birds. 'No, it's for you.' As soon as we started eating, two dogs appeared – their daughter's – and stared at us. But no sign of the daughter. 'She mixed herself a potion of herbs and was feeling a bit light-headed afterwards,' Elizabeth explained.

The Bullivants enjoyed (and I hope Elizabeth still enjoys) their garden, and that shines through. It isn't done for display for the public, following the currently accepted fashions, as so many seem to be, but, besides fuelling the business, to please themselves. That, in the long run, is also the best way to please the rest of us.

KINGSTON MAURWARD

—⟫•◦•⟪—

IF YOU SAID that the gardens at Kingston Maurward were large and impersonal, you would have a point. But they are also full of interest, both for their design and for their planting, and they owe as much to what has been going forward in them during the past ten years or less as to their historical associations of two and a half centuries.

The Palladian house belongs to them obliquely. Its classicism is discouraging. Built of brick around 1720, it was entirely faced in Portland stone seventy years later. Four specimens of *Magnolia grandiflora* trained against the garden front seem entirely appropriate to the setting. On this side the garden slopes down to an artificial lake in eighteenth-century landscape style.

The formal gardens lie on higher ground to one side and they are Edwardian in flavour, with much Portland stone in evidence (the quarries are only eight miles away), for paving, walls and balustrading. And very handsome, too. This was the work of the Hanbury family (even more famous for their garden at La Mortola, on the French/Italian Riviera), immediately after the First World War. Virtual dereliction followed when the site was taken over by the armed forces during the Second World War. Dorset County Council bought the estate in 1947 and their College of Agriculture and Horticulture was founded then. Slow rehabilitation has been greatly speeded up, of recent years, with the present team, headed by Bob Wadey (a Brighton man) as head of horticulture and Nigel Hewish (a West Countryman) as head gardener. The team of six is very strong and includes no dead wood. This shows in the rapid progress made by the gardens even in the twelve months between my two visits – both with Fergus Garrett, who made useful notes on which I am drawing as well as my own.

Naturally the horticultural students do some of the work, but they need close supervision. Although this is an institution, it does not have an institutional feel, but it is grand and is a popular venue for wedding receptions, dressed for the occasion and displayed for photographs, on or in front of flights

View from the Brick Garden, planted similarly to the Terrace Garden beyond, with the Palladian house behind.

of steps. Definitely not an atmospheric garden with a personal aura, but friendly and well used. It is open to the public from Easter to October and there are lawns on which the local croquet club can learn and practise their arts.

Both Bob Wadey and Nigel Hewish received training at Cannington, the Somerset College of Horticulture, under the enthusiastic influence of Roy Cheek, who is passionate about half-hardy perennials and bedding plants. This has rubbed off on these two pupils, and the climate suits exotica here as on the north Somerset coast, Kingston Maurward being just outside Dorchester and only a little inland from the Dorset coast overlooking the English Channel.

Approaching the formal gardens from the direction of the house, the Balustrade Garden is totally enclosed, a rectangular pool its central feature. This was unusable on my first visit, but it now has a new concrete floor, treated with Cemcol water sealant; the concrete sides merely needed sealing. Paving is of Portland stone, but the two narrow parallel beds in a central position, divided by paving, have now been amalgamated into one with the sensible width of 12 feet, which gives much more space to play with and scope for the use of larger plants.

Two perennials that were particularly impressive, each forming a large group, were the deep blue *Salvia guaranitica*, a four-footer, and the sub-shrubby Cape figwort, *Phygelius capensis*, with terracotta-coloured penstemon-like flowers in wide panicles. You can cut this to the ground in winter or else merely trim it, as with the Californian tree poppy, *Romneya coulteri*. The hard cut-back results in a slightly later flowering but I prefer it for producing very strong, basal growth and because it allows the opportunity, if you want to take it, of overplanting a colony with early-flowering bulbs.

There are excellent colonies, hanging over a low retaining wall, of prostrate rosemary, which I find too tender even for my reasonably mild Sussex climate. An impressive, free-standing tree of *Magnolia grandiflora* occupies one corner. Otherwise the perimeter consists largely of long-in-the-tooth sheltering shrubs; some are being replaced and others (like the bladder senna, *Colutea arborescens*) need to and doubtless will be.

Here, as elsewhere, there is a good deal of bedding out, which was the last to be done, in early June. It includes a banana species, *Musa ensete* (now *Ensete ventricosum*), which can be quickly raised from seed to a usable size and then lifted at the end of the season, potted up and saved under glass for another year. But it is a character of this and some other bananas that they keep on growing taller and cannot be cut back without killing the plant. The much dwarfer Japanese *Musa basjoo*, by contrast, makes sucker shoots from the base, which renders it more manageable and allows of vegetative propagation by division.

The (generally) tender, softly shrubby Paris daisies of the genus *Argyranthemum* are much in evidence, stock being annually renewed from cuttings. Here it was *A. gracile* that caught my attention, with its open habit, fine stems and leaves and small white daisies generously produced and carrying on well through the summer (when many argyranthemums take a rest).

Stock of a range of cannas is being rapidly built up. Some varieties new to Kingston Maurward had been acquired from Wisley at the end of a growing season. Instead of resting them through the winter, as would be normal practice, they were split into single crowns, each being potted and kept growing under heated glass. As soon as new shoots were formed, they were split again and then yet a third time, so that by the arrival of the planting-out season, quite a number of plants of each variety were already available. This kind of professionalism is impressively evident here.

Another example, in the Balustrade Garden, concerns the planting of each of several 'traditional' orange tubs with a large specimen of angel's trumpets, *Brugmansia (Datura) suaveolens*. These are grown in a removable metal sleeve, which overwinters under heated glass, but can simply (with the necessary manpower) be dropped into position for display on summer's return. However, I put 'traditional' into inverted commas because the tubs in question, made by the students, are of quite the wrong proportions, being too tall and too narrow. Furthermore, they have been treated with wood preservative and stain so as to be dark, shiny brown. This stands out most disagreeably. I was told that garden seats are to be made and treated in like manner, to create a feeling of unity. However, more recent news is that the tubs have now been removed to the Dragon Garden near to the nursery.

Framing the entrance to the Balustrade Garden are two bedded-out borders with an interesting low hedge edging doing the duty normally allotted to box. It was of the pale green and yellowish conifer, *Thuja plicata* 'Zebrina'. The hedging was quite old and in good order; it made me question why we are so wedded to the almost invariable choice of box for this purpose. There must be many conifers and perhaps a few other evergreens, like sarcococca, that would perform the same function just as well and make a change.

Outside the Balustrade Garden and against its high, south-facing wall is the Balustrade Border, planted for summer effect with a lively range of annuals and summer bedders. In early summer the chief contributions are made by small-flowered things like the mauve *Nemesia fruticans*, scarlet *Alonsoa warscewiczii*, *Nicotiana* 'Lime Green' and *Argyranthemum* 'Jamaica Primrose'. But the larger elements gradually take over, notably *Musa ensete*, various strains

The Balustrade Border, planted for subtropical effect with bananas (*Musa ensete*, now *Ensete ventricosum*), castor oil (*Ricinus*) and *Nicotiana sylvestris*.

of green- or bronze-leaved castor oil, *Ricinus communis*, pink, carmine and white *Cosmos bipinnatus* and the inestimable *Nicotiana sylvestris* (which features so often in these pages), with its large, pale green paddle leaves and stately inflorescences of long-tubed white blossom, deliciously night-scented. Balustrading and a broad flight of stone steps make a fine setting for such plants as these.

The steps take you up to the Terrace Garden, which is a considerable area and consists of a broad, central gravel walk flanked by lawns in which are set a series of oblong beds. Tulips and myosotis (forget-me-nots) were tried out in these but the tulips went down so badly to fire disease (a botrytis) that I doubt whether this expensive exercise will be continued. Sterilization of the soil with Dazomet would undoubtedly mitigate the trouble, as it would kill the soil-borne fungus spores, but wet springs (and this is a high rainfall area) would bring it back. So the beds concentrated on summer bedding. The interesting colour scheme emphasizes pink (*Verbena* 'Silver Anne'), blue, mauve and purple (*Ageratum* 'Blue Horizon', *Verbena rigida*, *Salvia farinacea* 'Victoria', *Nemesia fruticans*), white, and pale yellow (argyranthemums embrace various suitable colours), but above all the sharp interjection made by strongly spiky, pale yellow antirrhinums in a seed strain called 'Liberty Yellow'. This is sown in February and eventually potted individually into 4-inch pots. Nothing is left to chance here, and every plant to be used is given the full treatment.

Above the terrace and overlooking the Balustrade Garden is the Rose Garden, with geometric beds set in grass. The light alkaline soil at Kingston

The bedding-out terrace with very original plantings. Spires of *Antirrhinum* 'Liberty Yellow' provide firm accents.

Maurward does not suit roses well. Topsoil was brought in, to a depth of 18 inches, from the site of new car-parks. Each bed is devoted to one variety of Hybrid Tea or Floribunda rose, and every time the variety is changed – once in five years at longest – so is the soil. This is both a teaching institution, remember, and a display garden, so faltering roses simply would not do. However, they are not concerned with the varieties grown being the latest novelties. A full spray programme is maintained, fungicide being applied fortnightly through the growing season, insecticide when aphids show up. Growing roses well is hellish but we (not I) still make ourselves slaves to them.

On my first visit, the rose that appealed to me the most was 'Margaret Merril', an HT/Floribunda, blush white with several rows of petals and an open centre that still looked good in the fully-blown flower. That was in its first year from planting and it looked really strong and happy. A year later, it was faltering and sickly. Why? Heaven knows, but I'd guess that it was for the high jump.

At right angles to the far end of the Rose Garden is a double border of bedding penstemons, a National Collection, though correct naming is still, in many cases, a toss-up, even following the penstemon trial at Wisley. There were so many contradictions in the naming of plants submitted that it was hard to determine authenticity (I was on the judging committee and thus well aware of the snags). Some penstemons will come through the winter (depending on its severity), others not, but for the sake of uniformity of performance it is found advisable to renew and replant the entire stock

annually. Cuttings for plants to be bedded out in the following spring are taken in July.

I must say that to see all the varieties of a soft-textured plant such as this herded together is by no means an ideal method of display nor a good example to the public of how to use them in their own gardens. The excuse always given is that if all grown together they are the more easily compared.

By now you are overlooking the three croquet lawns, all in series on one big lawn, and this has high dry walling on two sides. The longer side comprises a rock garden, which I did not study as it looked uninteresting in high summer. Then comes a quarter-circular corner flight of steps – a charming feature, interlaced with the pink and white flowers of the self-sowing Mexican daisy, *Erigeron karvinskianus*. Next to this, a high retaining wall in part of which *Ceratostigma plumbaginoides* has, with its suckering habit, crept through the cracks over a large area, forming a curtain of deep blue in late summer and early autumn, followed by a fiery change of leaf colour. I have only once elsewhere seen it treated in this way (usually it makes ground cover), but it looks smashing.

Arrived at the garden's highest point, there is a vista, looking outwards, along an avenue of purple beeches. The motto of this piece of garden is to be

Left, A carefully considered bedding scheme with argyranthemums, diascias, heliotrope and *Verbena rigida*.

Right, The traditional herbaceous border. Red hot pokers against rambler rose 'American Pillar'; potentillas, golden rod and *Achillea filipendulina*.

red and largely contributed by cannas. Old features include a delightful stone summerhouse, the steps leading down from which finish in a sliver of pond that runs across the line of vision. That's good; the summerhouse roof is covered with white-flowered *Sedum album*, which is a weed when growing in competitive situations but ideal here.

At the pond's other end, new steps rise to a newly constructed circular temple which looks over much of the more formal garden areas, most of them enclosed by yew hedging and including a fair sprinkling of yew topiary. Although old, the yews were looking noticeably vigorous and lusty on my second visit. For the first time, they had all been fed, in late winter, with a slow release Osmacote fertilizer. It is more easily applied than dusty fish, blood and bone, which we have been using for many years in my garden. Two 25-kilo bags at £50 per bag had seen the job through. I shall change over.

A box 'lawn' has been planted on the rise leading up to the temple – a mat of low box bushes kept clipped to make an even upper surface (cherry laurels have been treated elsewhere in similar style, though on a larger scale). I should have tried plants with more interesting foliage, myself. In any case, more than one clone of box has been planted, which is a frequently occurring accident but fatal, as there is always variation in vigour as between the clones. The temple itself is raw and crude. It was made in conjunction with Weymouth College, a further education establishment which runs a stonemason's course in support of the Portland stone industry. A worthy cause is not necessarily synonymous with good design or workmanship.

Continuing the tour, a principal feature is a little circular yew-enclosed garden in which niches are cut for statues. The paths are brick-paved, so it is called the Brick Garden. It otherwise consists of a formal arrangement of informally planted beds, in the same style and colouring as the Terrace Garden, on to which it looks, with the house at the far end of the vista. It is charming, though I might be tempted to try some different plantings.

It leads on to double Traditional Herbaceous Borders. There is a double row, on tripods, along the back of these (with yew hedging for a background), of 'American Pillar' rambler roses. This is the brightest shade of carmine pink in the palette. Colouring, overall, is unfashionably brilliant, which makes an invigorating change from the good taste school. *Achillea filipendulina* 'Gold Plate' and scarlet *Lychnis chalcedonica* are in unashamed juxtaposition with the rose. In an all-herbaceous border, I miss the variation in form and texture which an admixture of shrubs would contribute. The best contrasts were provided by groups of *Artemisia lactiflora*, which does have style and substance, with its dark, pinnate foliage, crowned by creamy plumes.

You pass by amorphous plantings of 'old' roses, which leave me cold, into the Crown Garden, circular again, the top of the enclosing yew hedging cut into crenellations. Sweet Williams and foxgloves are later replaced by salvias from the National Collection, also held here. Many salvias are unworthy of garden space, so our team is becoming more selective with the years. Four central crescents are planted with *Geranium sanguineum*, the bloody cranesbill. It gets sprawly, mid-season, and is then cut back to grow again. It is edged with *Liriope muscari*, whose grape hyacinth-like mauve spikes are at their best in autumn.

When you get back to the lawns sloping down to the lake on the south side of the house, you will find that they are richly decked, either side of a permanently mown central sweep, with spring-flowering bulbs. The lake, which is a dammed stream, is fed by nitrogen-rich water leached from farmland above it, and this can cause trouble with unsightly algae covering much of the surface in summer. It seemed much improved on my second visit, which is possibly due to the use of barley straw bales at the inlet through which the water is forced to pass. This magic, not yet fully decoded, is being increasingly practised and researched without yet being adequately explained.

The walk along the lakeside, called Armistice Walk as it was made soon after the 1918 Armistice, goes past a Japanese Garden, in the making when I saw it. There is a stream along the back of this garden, and the steep, treed bank behind it has ivy for ground cover interrupted by huge clumps of the hart's-tongue fern, *Phyllitis scolopendrium*. All this is wild and untouched by civilizing influences; it does have a strong appeal.

One of the noblest deciduous trees is the oriental plane, or chenar, *Platanus orientalis*, which forms the centrepiece and meeting place in so many Asian villages. In our climate, it is apt to have divided trunks, often separate and forming a colony, as at Blickling Hall, in Norfolk. They have a magnificent specimen, some 200 years old, by the lakeside at Kingston Maurward, its branches sweeping down almost to the ground, so that you can admire its big palmate leaves with their long, acute points and shining finish. This has a single bole; another, by its side, has divided into two, but is still a fine tree.

Here, below the lake, the original Elizabethan manor house is just above you. There are a couple of lusty young tulip trees on the slope leading up to the Elizabethan Walled Garden, which is bedded and is also a demonstration garden. The work area and glasshouse units are also situated here.

With all the bedding-out that this garden entails, many people might throw up their hands in horror at the labour and costs involved. They would be quite wrong to do so. Bedding is a long practised art that can be done badly (plenty of examples of that) or well. It is capable of refinement in many ways and has developed amazingly since Victorian times. Not only have we many more suitable species and cultivated varieties to choose from but our concepts of how to present them attractively are improving all the time.

Neither is it as expensive as you might think. Seed is relatively cheap to buy; often it can be home-saved. Vegetatively propagated bedding plants can be manufactured on site from cuttings. In terms of input, outlay is cheap. Labour, of course, is not, but the gardens are deservedly attracting an ever-increasing section of the paying public, and there is plenty of room for them. It is not a garden, like Sissinghurst, that is likely to be worn out by feet.

My one fear, speaking as a gardener, is that, having found a winning formula, as for instance in the terrace planting, it will be stuck to and quickly become traditional. This kind of ephemeral gardening gives the greatest opportunities for change – rapid change – and for the implementation of new ideas. It is all very well to be thinking more in terms of new themes and features, like the Japanese Garden, which will interest students as projects, but flexibility and change in established areas is, in the long run, even more important. Yet older features are apt to be taken for granted. They never should be.

I should hate to leave this garden in any way that sounded downbeat. Bob Wadey and Nigel Hewish are admirably hard-working and efficient, undaunted by any sort of challenge, but they also, clearly, have an excellent relationship. They enjoy life and I bet they find occasion for plenty of good laughs. Small wonder they head a happy and effective team.

OVERBECKS

———◦———

GOOD WEATHER certainly makes a difference when you're travelling and looking at gardens, however we may tell ourselves that they are beautiful in the rain, as, indeed, they can be. But the comfort and luxury of feeling happy and relaxed are not to be gainsaid.

As during the whole of our West Country tour at the start of May, the weather was perfect, like early summer yet with the freshness of spring. Fergus and I left Puncknowle after quite an early breakfast, as we were warned of a two-hour drive to reach Overbecks, which is way off the beaten track to Cornwall and is right at the southern tip of Devon.

All the same, the temptation, within ten minutes of leaving the Old Rectory, to pause was irresistible. Below us on our left, as we headed for Bridport, was a shingly beach, entirely deserted except for one car. If one car, why not two? Such is the gregarious instinct of humanity. But I am unfair. We would have gone down that tempting track to the beach had it been empty, and perhaps even if we'd had to walk, although time was on our conscience.

It was wonderful there, the morning so fresh, the shadows long, although the sun was warm and there were great splodges of seakale, sunbathing on the beach. Crinkly young leaves still flushed with purple, the open-clustered flowers stretched out beyond them. Naturally we had to drop to our knees to breathe in their honey scent.

Fergus, being a champion stone-thrower, exercised his art into the expectant sea. That diversion was one of the best moments in the trip.

The signposts to Overbecks still read Sharpitor. That was its name until the vanity of Mr Otto Overbeck, its last private owner, demanded as a condition of its bequeathal to the National Trust that its name be changed to commemorate himself.

The approach, along a narrow river valley to the west side of Salcombe Bay, was all brown and blighted, still (on 2 May), by the frost which had

The view out to Salcombe Bay from the garden, with spires of *Echium pininana* in the foreground.

smitten south, central and west England on the night of 4/5 April, following a spring of exceptional earliness. The we-shall-pay-for-it-later prophets of doom had been proved right. I thought the excitements of February and March were well worth an April frost, myself. Living dangerously makes you enjoy all the more keenly the highlights which you know to be ephemeral.

But, rounding the corner of the bay to Overbecks itself, all was smiling and unharmed. You hear the sea lapping the cliffs below you; it is as near as that. Radiation frosts don't stand a chance. That is not to say that severe winters never affect those parts; they do and did in the series ending in 1987. But what seems disastrous at the time is soon forgotten. Recovery in this soft climate is quick, and some kinds of damage even prove a blessing. A *Drimys winteri* at Overbecks had grown so large as to flower against the sky, where you could scarcely see it. After it had been chopped back, almost to ground level, it sprouted with amazing vigour and its great bunches of waxy white blossom were flaunting at eye and nose level at the time of our visit.

Mr Tony Murdoch, the head gardener, took us round. He is an exceptional gardener and, were it not for him, I should have little to say about this garden, apart from its most obvious features.

Being a National Trust garden gives it security but it has so far avoided the institutionalized stamp of so many NT properties. In part this is because the terrain around here is very steep, sometimes cliff-like. There is not the space for many visiting cars. There were 30,000 visitors in 1989 and that is about as many as the place can take. It is not many by NT standards but they are not anxious to encourage any more to come, with the attendant problems of overcrowding.

And, being in this cul-de-sac, Tony Murdoch has largely been left to get on with the job and do as he sees fit. He correctly describes this as an adventurous garden and it reflects his adventurous spirit.

The property had three owners. It was started in 1901 by Mr Edric Hopkins, who constructed the very necessary terracing, and was extended to its present size by Mr and Mrs Vereker between 1913 and 1928 when the property was sold to the eponymous Overbeck. (There is still, however, a fuchsia to commemorate the previous name of Sharpitor. When going round the garden with Tony Murdoch, Chris Brickell noticed a green and white variegated branch sport on *Fuchsia magellanica* 'Molinae', green-leaved with pale pink flowers. Tony propagated it and it is now widely circulated as 'Sharpitor'.)

Overbecks has magnificent views over Salcombe Bay. In one of the best, the water is framed by a golden *Cupressus macrocarpa* on the left and Chusan palms, *Trachycarpus fortunei*, on the right. They are typical coastal features in this part of the country. The palms are remarkably hardy but they give the right exotic

Left, Kniphofias and *Crocosmia* 'Lucifer'.

Right, The exciting inflorescences of *Beschorneria yuccoides*.

touch to seaside resorts. At Overbecks there is one quaint semi-woodland planting where the trees are all palms, while the ground flora, at the time of our visit, consisted of bluebells, daisies (*Bellis*) and the white *Allium* that is so widely naturalized in the south-west, *A. triquetrum*. Among these, already in early May, were interspersed a few scarlet spikes of *Kniphofia* – red hot pokers. One wished for more, but kniphofias don't generally come on till June.

Magnolias were much planted in the early years, notably, in 1901, a vast pink *Magnolia campbellii*, its stems beautifully wrapped and felted in green moss. This tree species often leaves you with a stiff neck, trying to get a view of it against the sky, but here, thanks to the terracing and steep descent, you can admire it at eye level – but that's in March or even February, before many people are around and, of course, it is desperately vulnerable to rough weather. You have to be there on the right day, rather than the right week, photograph it, as has Tony Murdoch, and then live on your photographs for the rest of the year – or of a lifetime.

As is so often the way in old gardens owned by amateurs who prefer to turn a blind eye to plants that have become eyesores rather than take decisive action by grubbing and replanting, Overbecks was full of clutter when Tony took office nearly twenty years ago. There were periwinkles and leathery bergenias all through the garden, the inevitable evergreen *Euonymus japonicus* of seaside suburbs, hamamelis and other winter-flowering shrubs without summer appeal, and much more run-of-the-mill parks stuff.

The mainstay of Tony's plantings are boldly handsome foliage plants of exotic appearance. I completely fell for astelias, here; *Astelia nervosa* and *A. chathamica*, which seems to be no different from the New Zealand nursery firm's 'Silver Spear' – doubtless a better-selling name. There are lots of good spiky-leaved plants and this had a young, pale-purple-leaved cordyline behind it. The criss-crossing of all their strap leaves was compounded by the criss-crossing of their shadows in the morning sunshine.

A planting of this kind needs renewing, unless it is entirely to change its character, within a few years, because the cordyline, from looking a fairly well-mannered explosion close to ground level, will grow into a tree with a stout trunk, if simply left. That's fine in the right context (I am thinking of a cordyline avenue at Logan, in south-west Scotland), but an active and well-trained gardener with a streak of the necessary ruthlessness acquired in the course of his, or her, profession will be prepared to discipline the changes within an assemblage of living plants, all the time.

Another astelia planting had the steely shimmer of *A. nervosa* 'Red Gem' against the jazzy pink- and green-striped spears of a New Zealand flax, *Phormium tenax* 'Firebird'. In a wall behind, the soft haze of colonizing *Erigeron karvinskianus*, that obliging little Mexican daisy which fills in so charmingly if given a lead to get it started.

Fleshy *Agave americana* and its boldly cream-variegated version are generally hardy here. Of one backdrop, where they have been planted in a high retaining wall, Fergus remarked that their leaves 'stick out like the blades on Boadicea's chariot wheels'. The walls themselves, incidentally, are beautifully made with dressed grey stone from local cliffs.

Another exciting foliage plant (I am tempted to give it a whirl myself) is *Beschorneria yuccoides*. It makes a yucca-like rosette of moderately stiff leaves, but the inflorescence – half a dozen to a good clump – is its main point, and this, with its large, bright pink bracts ('flesh pink, almost an uncomfortable colour, reminding of squashed rabbits on the road' – Fergus) had newly expanded. There were plenty of these amazing plants and they continually draw the eye.

So does *Echium pininana*, both at the juvenile, lance-leaved rosette stage and when it runs up its 20-foot flower spikes. More on that in my Isle of Wight chapter. I think the bushy *E. fastuosum*, at 4 feet or so, a more clubbable plant. Its stubby, terminal blue spikes went well, at Overbecks, with the beschornerias and I have seen them even more arrestingly presented, in Australia (West Victoria), with white arum lilies, *Zantedeschia aethiopica*, and also, near Christchurch in New Zealand, with the yellow blossom of a shrubby senecio and the white daisies of *Argyranthemum foeniculaceum*. This Canary Isles echium, exotic cousin to our native viper's bugloss of the sea shore, has got around the world and naturalizes readily.

Pittosporums can grow enormous in a climate like Overbecks', but a foliage grouping of Tony Murdoch's that appealed to me used quite low ingredients with the variegated *Pittosporum tenuifolium* 'Silver Queen' behind a lower-growing clone, *P.t.* 'Tom Thumb' (three of these) and an apron of grey-leaved gazanias in front. 'Silver Queen' was a young plant, only a few feet tall. 'Tom Thumb' is apt to look smug and dumpy, but the informal grouping saved it from this. Its young foliage is green, set off bizarrely, though pleasantly enough, by the purple mature foliage on older shoots. The gazanias would be a blaze of blossom later on but were doing a good job as foliage plants at this early season.

Gazanias are daisies, and daisies (composites) of one kind or another are a major theme at Overbecks. *Anthemis cupaniana* makes large, loose grey mats and looked comfortable weaving around the base of spiky plants like phormiums and fascicularias. It was seething with white, yellow-centred daisies in early May.

Most of us can grow that, but we are less relaxed about osteospermums, euryops and argyranthemums. We expect or half expect to lose them in the winter, and therefore treat them as half-hardy bedding plants. This often means that we miss their very best moment as garden plants, when they expand their first great rush of blossom at winter's end.

Osteospermum 'Lady Leitrim', wide open to May sunshine.

Many of these shrubby composites are naturally short day flowerers (like the florist's chrysanthemums). They may flower a bit during the summer, but long days and short nights promote vegetative growth in them rather than blossom initiation. Breeding and selection have reduced this tendency in quite a number of recent clones, but the fact remains that they tend to give of their best in spring. But to benefit from this, you need large, well-established colonies that have overwintered in your garden.

Thus, the pale yellow *Osteospermum* 'Buttermilk', planted out in April or May as pot-grown specimens overwintered under glass, will flower enough, perhaps (though sometimes not), to make you feel the exercise was worthwhile, but are as nothing to the ecstatic display laid on, as at Overbecks, by plants that have been growing outside for a year or three (they do need renewing with young stock fairly frequently, though a stiff cut-back often does the trick of rejuvenation).

There are many different osteospermums here and it does give your heart a bound of pleasure to see crowds of them expanded so joyfully (one cannot help being anthropomorphic) to the sunshine. There was a handsome grouping of a pale, sub-shrubby osteospermum, 'Brickell's Hybrid', next to an early-flowering bearded iris, but the osteospermum that probably appealed to us the most was 'Lady Leitrim' (who she?). It has long, narrow white rays, slightly arching and with spaces between them – a spider flower but with many more legs than eight.

A large bush of *Euryops pectinata*, with bright (but not brash) yellow daisies against finely cut grey leaves in rosettes, made 'a splendid corner piece . . . and really anchors the wall behind', in Fergus's words. I planted out a good-sized specimen of this, one spring. It grew prodigiously all summer and might have been described as a good foliage plant but I wanted its flowers, in vain. My one criticism of this euryops (apart from the fact that I can't grow it the way they do on the south coast) is that it holds on to its old flower-heads after the rays have shrivelled and browned. It is the same with *E. chrysanthemoides*. Ideally, you should dead-head them at frequent intervals.

Then there are the argyranthemums, which we used to lump under *Chrys-anthemum*; the Paris daisy, *Argyranthemum frutescens*, and close relations. Again they flower most freely in the shorter days of spring and autumn. I took special pleasure in the stabbing contrast between *A. foeniculaceum*, with lacy, glaucous leaves and white daisies, close to the tulip poppy, *Papaver commutatum*, an annual with blood red flowers and large black blotches at the petal bases.

Although we were there in spring, Tony Murdoch is greatly interested in plants whose high season is late summer and autumn, a season which, he rightly thinks, is given insufficient attention in the majority of gardens.

In the Statue Garden, whose central feature is a bronze known as *First Flight*, described as being 'delightful' in the guide – I have no recollection of it whatsoever – there are four long rectangular beds in a formal design but informally planted (often the best treatment). They were full of shrubby junk on Tony's arrival but he has replanted with interesting herbaceous perennials. The hemerocallis would not, I have to say, be my first choice; their foliage is tedious, once they have flowered. But there are many perennials which most of us would consider tender (not always correctly), but which receive and respond to hardy plant treatment here.

For instance, cannas, their foliage always an asset even when not flowering. The vigorous, cut-leaved *Dahlia merckii*, with small single mauve flowers on a rangy plant, can be hardy even in Perthshire. 'Bishop of Llandaff', also fern-leaved but purple in this case, has crimson red flowers and is planted near *Crocosmia* 'Lucifer', which is fiery, volcanic red. They must look good together in July. Argyranthemums, already flowering in spring, would have an extended season, and there is *Kniphofia caulescens*, whose evergreen rosettes of glaucous foliage are more sustaining than its coral flower spikes in early autumn.

There is a range of herbaceous salvias, here. The deep blue *Salvia patens*,

The borders in summer, with blue agapanthus, kniphofias, crinums, dahlias and annual sunflowers.

with tuberous roots, is moderately hardy (rather in the dahlia category) and so is *S. involucrata* 'Bethellii', which grows to 3 feet and has flowers and bracts in shocking pinky mauve. A good plant. *S. rutilans*, with its strong pineapple aroma, is hardy here, though not for most of us, and the same applies to *S. fulgens*, whose red flowers on a tall plant can make a magnificent display in autumn if capsids haven't attacked the growing shoots. Not unlike these is *Lobelia tupa*, growing like a cabbage when I saw it. Later it carries long racemes of two-lipped, sulky red blossom. Unlike the statue, it is a plant no gardener could overlook. There are blue agapanthus to set it and the red salvias off.

Overbecks starts with the huge advantage of its almost too-good-to-be-true setting. But this is also a plantsman's garden and one, moreover, where the plants are arranged so as to help each other, which is cause for added inspiration. I want to visit again, in autumn.

THE GARDEN HOUSE

—————◆—————

FROM OVERBECKS, soon after midday, we drove cross-country to the Garden House, Buckland Monachorum, losing our way among slag heaps of china clay. Then, the other side of Yelverton, which is the nearest town, we lost ourselves again, for lack of helpful signs. We had come the 'wrong' way; had we approached from Plymouth (so we were assured) or from the north, we should have met clear signing.

The Garden House receives only 6,000 or so visitors a year, although open every day from noon to 5.00 p.m., April to September. Perhaps not easily finding it is one reason. Lack of National Trust advantages is another.

This property is close to the Devon–Cornwall border on its west side and to Dartmoor to the east. The house, at the top of a steep walled-in slope, which is the main part of the garden, was a vicarage built in 1826. But the site is of ancient habitation, going back to the thirteenth century at least. A tower at the lowest level is an earlier feature, part of a previous vicarage. The barn, the stone walls and the four terraces which take up the steep gradient also date back a long way.

Within this walled area (you couldn't have called it a garden) was nothing but rubbish when Lionel Fortescue bought the property in 1946. He showed me round in 1958, which was my first visit and the only one in his lifetime. Once a classics master at Eton College, where he had the reputation of a martinet, he was not a lovable man but he needed friends and made them, especially, of young men. Most good gardeners are rather nice people, in my experience. You wouldn't have called Fortescue nice but he had excellent taste and a passion for plants and gardening.

Michael Hickson, who has been head gardener at Knightshayes Court for well over twenty years, trained under him and, in 1978, three years before he died, Fortescue took Keith Wiley into his employ, together with Ros, his hard-working wife, and they are still there, running the gardens and adjoining

The lower garden from the top of the tower.

Plant Centre, which offers many rare plants. This was just about the best thing that could have happened.

I first met Keith when he was a horticultural student at Wye College, Kent (University of London). Tom Wright, his lecturer, brought him and his fellow students to see my garden and I was unforgettably impressed by his receptiveness and keenness to learn.

Fortescue founded a trust to keep his garden going and Tom Wright, who brought me on my first, 1958, visit, is one of its management committee members. Running a garden by committee is not very satisfactory, however delightful the members. In the last resort, whatever its individuals may think, it has to come to consensus decisions. As Keith says, ninety per cent of gardening is hard slog; the last ten per cent is the cream which makes it all worth while – the planning for change and improvement. If the gardener on the spot has it in him, or her, to do this effectively, then the garden remains a personal one; if not, it becomes institutional. On the whole, I think Keith gets his way a good deal of the time, but he has a strong personality and compromise is possibly not his strongest suit.

Of course, gardens of detailed interest are expensive to run, let alone to expand, and, unless it can generate surplus income, inflation can bring a charitable trust that seemed generous when founded to its knees. The Fortescue Trust is on a sticky wicket.

This is, indeed, a plantsman's garden and full of surprises, but pruning and shaping play a major role here. 'Shape is everything,' said Keith. 'It's with you all the year.' (He would probably have said the same, with equal emphasis, of colour, had that been the subject of our conversation, or of year-round interest; the most important things are the ones at the front of your mind at any given moment.)

Pruning and shaping are a way of life in Japanese gardening, arising in large part from being so short of habitable space on those overcrowded, volcanic islands. Without aping their gardens, which never works properly given our totally different cultures, there is still a great deal we can learn from them.

Hoheria glabrata with delphiniums.

For example, *Magnolia* × *loebneri* 'Merrill' is normally seen as a large, shapeless lump of a shrub. 'Needs no pruning' is the accepted precept for magnolia care. Keith has trained his into a graceful spire whose shape is retained by pruning it early enough during the summer for it to make new shoots on which to set flower buds, during the remainder of the growing season.

Removal of Fortescue's vast Leyland cypress hedges, 30 or 40 feet high and gobbling up all the moisture and nutrients within that distance of their trunks, has opened up new views and vistas. One of these is terminated by a mature purple beech (a huge, carmine-flowered *arboreum* rhododendron looks super with this as its background). Keith has made a path leading up towards it, but a 10-foot tall colony of *Pieris japonica taiwanensis* would have blocked the vista. Simple. By first cutting it back and then pinching out all its young vertical shoots, he restricts it to a 4-foot cushion and it flowers abundantly at that level.

Out by the drive there are large specimens, beneath trees, of *Viburnum plicatum* 'Mariesii', each 18 feet wide but now only 4 feet high. Again, by pinching back, he has retained space between the viburnums and the branches above them.

The lower garden around barn and tower was a cobbled courtyard from which Fortescue removed all the hardcore, replacing it with topsoil. It is planted in a cottage garden style, but structural features are kept neatly trimmed by frequent clipping, preventing it from all growing into an amorphous mess. Given a firm framework, many plants can be allowed to self-sow and do their own thing – apparently, anyway, even if control is never far removed.

Looking eastwards from the tower (good views from the top of this), there is a double line of clipped false cypresses, *Chamaecyparis lawsoniana* 'Columnaris Glauca' (conifers and ferns vie with each other for the most complex pseudo-botanical names); then a thin tall line of *Cotoneaster lacteus* curves round to the left and this is kept razor sharp with two or three annual trimmings.

Beyond that the garden appears to be peopled with specimen bushes, many of them conifers, clipped into cone shapes. I have to say I find these fussy. Given the size of the garden I feel that broader effects, more restful on the eye, are needed. Here we have too much incident. Keith has not yet come around to feeling the presence created by bamboos, although, on a smaller scale, he is fully aware of clump-forming and tufted grasses in the same role, using *Stipa arundinacea* as a corner piece. Its brown flowers are beautiful in late summer and autumn.

When I say that I find this a difficult garden to photograph, I think this is because it lacks cohesion. Either you are taking it in panoramically, including a lovely borrowed landscape beyond the walls (something that Fortescue hardly noticed), or you are looking at detailed plantings, many of them of great beauty and interest.

Keith is aware of the importance of resting points, views and lookouts as you go round the garden, however. A view of the tower from the centre of the Bowling Green terrace, which is the second terrace down, has a low foreground of *Rhodohypoxis*, while the bay around this seat is planted all in shades of yellow, largely of foliage.

Keith Wiley loves working with stone, and on the south side of the walled garden, looking across to the barn and tower, he has built a roomy, round seat enclosed in low stone walling. And he has rebuilt the lookout from the north end of the top terrace.

Camellias and rhododendrons enjoy this moist climate with its 60 inches of annual rainfall. As garden features, he has no higher an opinion of camellias than I have. Their flowers are scattered 'blob, blob, blob like a child trying for the first time to draw a flowering bush'. But clipped camellia hedges (they don't flower a lot) along the margin of the top (Annexe) terrace help to promote a feeling, here, of enclosure, secrecy and romance. Into one of them, a circular moongate has been shaped so that you get a sudden view out to the tower.

Otherwise the top terrace was planted by Fortescue with yellow azaleas, to which has been added a background of laburnums, and the yellow-leaved birch, *Betula* 'Golden Cloud', ends one view along this curved path. The azaleas, 'Golden Oriole', 'Sunbeam' and 'Toucan', are all in soft shades. In 'Toucan' the flowers are margined in pink. Pink and yellow can blend happily and do so here.

The brown, grass-like *Carex buchananii* with the tiny white stars of *Arenaria balearica. Hosta fortunei* 'Albopicta' behind.

Japanese maples are another group that enjoy the acid soil and damp climate. *Acer palmatum* 'Butterfly' has a pretty pink variegation while 'Beni-Tsukasa' is coral pink throughout and, at 6 feet, is lovely seen with the sun shining through it.

There are many happy details and groupings of which I must mention a few. For instance, an undulating bed of deep green moss, *Polytrichum commune*; just that, and it does not, here at least, require overhead shading.

Grasses and grass-like plants are much appreciated. The New Zealand *Libertia peregrinans* is warm olive green and ochreous orange in its stiff, evergreen spear leaves at all times, especially in winter, but the 'Gold Leaf' clone which I met here for the first time is brighter still.

I grow Bowles's golden sedge, *Carex elata* 'Aurea', which is a cheerful feature from May to August, both in my pond and in a damp border, but again new to me was a selection of another native, the greater pond sedge, *Carex riparia*, called 'Variegata'. It has narrow green margins to a very pale, nearly white leaf. It reverts to the plain green type plant and has a pretty daunting running rootstock, but is a good plant so long as you know what to expect! And its black inflorescences are smart.

With its warm brown colouring, the tufted *Carex buchanani* is typical of New Zealand flora and doesn't in the least look dead (as its enemies proclaim) once you have noticed the healthy sheen on its narrow leaves. You find it, at the Garden House, with the mat-forming *Pratia pedunculata*, covered in its little pale blue lobelia-like flowers; *Arenaria balearica*, another mat-former, like a tight-growing moss above which hover its tiny, pure white flowers on thread-fine stalks; and, in the background, *Hosta fortunei* 'Albopicta', which has butter yellow and pale green variegation in the spring and lacks the hearty coarseness of 'Frances Williams' and similar broad-leaved types.

Uncinia rubra is a grass with luminous red leaves that you don't see around much. It self-sows, and as young plants look the freshest, you can easily turn over your stock.

Different shapes and colours in leaves are thoughtfully combined: hostas, rodgersias, grasses, filipendulas (with pinnate foliage) and polygonums (now persicarias). *Astelia nervosa* is pretty hardy here, and Keith pointed out that there are four different colours combined within its ribbed strap leaves. You can pick out any one of them with which to make your next plant association, using it.

There's one long-lasting summer planting that he is proud of. At a low level, two rambling plants, both tender perennials needing to be replanted each spring: *Bidens ferulifolia*, which has small yellow coreopsis-like flowers for many months, and *Helichrysum petiolare* 'Limelight', whose lime green, heart-shaped leaves never look better (unlike the greys) than when wet. It is saved from burning in the sun by a little overhead shade from a nearby acer. Behind these and at a higher level, where they are supported, at 2 feet, by horizontally stretched large-mesh wire netting, *Thalictrum delavayi* and *Geranium* 'Ann Folkard'. The thalictrum grows to 8 or 9 feet and carries large, airy panicles of mauve blossom. The cranesbill, which is another rambler and develops a terrific spread in the course of its May to October flowering season, is bright purple (not quite magenta) with a near black eye.

I can't grow the mossy saxifrages, *Saxifraga hypnoides*. Good-tempered though they are, the sparrows pick their cushions to pieces. A pretty combination here, however, linked a ribbon of pink saxifrage with the invading yellow-green foliage of golden creeping Jenny, *Lysimachia nummularia* 'Aurea'.

Drystone retaining walls, which are such a feature, give ample opportunities to colonizers in the cracks. One area has been taken over by the invasive (it can't get out of hand here) *Campanula poscharskyana*, whose pale blue stars are flowering at the same time as the white, cherry-blossom-like *Hoheria* 'Glory of Amlwch' in June–July. (Practise saying Amlwch before going public.)

Lilies-of-the-valley are, I had long realized, great colonizers of paving-

Euphorbia griffithii 'Fireglow' and white honesty, *Lunaria annua*.

stone cracks but I hadn't seen them in a vertical wall face before. Neither had I met the clone called 'Hardwick Hall', whose broad leaves have a thin, paler margin.

Keith Wiley is really excited about the coming years, and the changes he plans to make which will take in an area on the garden's north side from which the last of the Leyland cypresses have been extracted. He certainly deserves the opportunity to put them into execution.

POSTSCRIPT

Keith and Ros have been extremely energetic in the years that have elapsed since I visited. He writes: 'If the original creation of the garden by Mr and Mrs Fortescue was stage 1, then what happened in 1993 was an equally important stage 2 (of 3 stages) in our long-term aim of putting the Garden House at the very pinnacle of English Gardens.' Besides a new plant sales area, the size of the existing garden has, in effect, been quadrupled, making it 8 acres in all. I must go and have another look.

TREBAH

MAJOR ANTHONY HIBBERT (a retired gunner) received us most kindly at Trebah on the afternoon of 3 May, the weather still cloudless, windless. He and his wife bought this property in 1981. It had been through long periods of neglect during and after the last war, changing hands every few years – which is about the worst that can happen to a place.

But Tony Hibbert, albeit in his late seventies, is a man of great energy and he has brought this property back to pristine condition. He has, moreover, founded the Trebah Garden Trust as a registered charity, so as to provide security (in so far as this can be guaranteed) and continuity for this marvellous inheritance. He was hoping for 40,000 visitors in 1990, to provide very necessary income (this is what the Garden House needs), and there are a number of attractions aside from the garden itself, not least a children's adventure playground and a Friends of Trebah organization, whose members receive a number of privileges. There is also an adjoining nursery of rare plants suited to the Cornish climate.

All this Major Hibbert has initiated and I know that I should be acting similarly for my own home, but I lack this kind of organizational energy, while admiring it in others.

Trebah (pronounced *Tree*-ba, with the accent on the first syllable) is spectacular. From the modest eighteenth-century house you look down a 25-acre ravine which drops 200 feet to the sea, a part of the sheltered Helford River estuary. This is not far from Falmouth.

The Quaker family of Fox, who owned a great deal of property around here including the neighbouring Glendurgan, planted this valley garden essentially as we see it, in the mid-nineteenth century. Plantings do not last for ever, and the storm which swept most of England in January 1990 took toll of more than seventy trees here. People are always reluctant to cut down old trees that have obviously seen better days but are still valued companions, so

most of them have to wait upon acts of God to do the job and a messy old job He makes of it.

The garden looks south. From a broad sitting-out terrace on the house's garden front, the ground drops fairly precipitously and in order to steady the feeling that you're falling over the edge, Tony Hibbert constructed another terrace with huge boulders of weathered granite set into the ground in two layers by way of a retaining wall. These are a handsome feature. There is gravel between them which seems to invite the use of low basking plants like *Convolvulus cneorum* and the osteospermums and gazanias with other South African daisies, not to mention small bulbs like sparaxis, ixia and babiana.

To the west side of this terrace, the Major has channelled a stream to make a cascade, a grotto and a pool with colourful koi carp in it (they were sheltering from the heat of the afternoon sun beneath a ledge and had to be chivvied out with a stick to display themselves). There are some good plantings here, ferns and the primitive *Cyathea dealbata* contrasting with cordylines, the variegated agave, the shimmering silver grey strap leaves of *Astelia chathamica* and the rosettes of *Echium pininana*, one of which was soaring to 14 feet or more as it came into flower. Although modestly self-deprecating of his talents in this department, Tony Hibbert is an excellent gardener. Only the seat benches, here, were truly hideous, and worth photographing on that account. I made Fergus sit on one of them to give scale and he looked suitably grim. However, I gather that these eyesores are stop-gaps.

We now made our elliptical circuit of the ravine by the recommended route. I do find the kinds of plants that you can grow in these mild, maritime gardens, wherever there is shelter, very exciting, and there were many old friends here, like *Beschorneria yuccoides*, already noted at Overbecks.

You follow the stream bed where great colonies of arum lilies, *Zantedeschia aethiopica*, were already at their best. They naturalize here and you see them naturalized in many parts of the world, where they are often regarded as weeds, but the elegance of their inflorescence is of a sculptural beauty that custom will never stale, for me. They were well contrasted with *Libertia grandiflora*, again white-flowered and self-sowing but with spear leaves. And its flowers are roughly triangular, as with many *Iridaceae*.

I was delighted to see *Cyperus alternifolius*, which we know as a house plant about 18 inches tall, growing here to 6 feet in the open. Its radiating leaf spokes atop naked stems give it a skeletal presence. I frequently put it in my sunk garden pond for the summer and I have had self-sown seedlings in nearby paving cracks in the following year, as a result, but could never hope to overwinter an established plant outside.

There is a wonderful glade of tree ferns, *Dicksonia antarctica*, so delicate and

Build-up with agave (front), astelia, *Cordyline australis* and *Echium pininana* flowering against the sky.

The koi carp pool area with tree fern, *Dicksonia antarctica*. Fergus Garrett (not too happy).

yet so strong. They self-sow, which seems a great compliment. Wonderful shapes to have in a garden. So, of course, has *Gunnera manicata*; we are more accustomed to that but it is outsize at Trebah, growing 18 feet tall and with leaves 8 feet across.

Sasa palmata, albeit invasive, is a most effective bamboo with particularly broad leaves. It makes a dense thicket and really looks a lot handsomer if old canes are removed to keep a colony thinned out.

In any Cornish landscape garden you expect to see a great many rhododendrons, often growing to trees, and a good proportion of species and hybrids that would be too tender in south-east England. So it may sound a bit of an anticlimax in a plantsman's ears to say that the greatest impact on that day and a focal point for a great distance was made by the old hardy hybrid 'Cynthia'. You might expect to see it in any suburban garden, but never mind. Its rich magenta flower-heads make a deep impression (Fergus, whose tastes have not yet become jaded or refined by snob values, was thrilled), especially when displayed on an enormous specimen in keeping with the scale of this garden. At Belsay Hall in Northumberland (see page 122) it makes a similar impact.

The florists' 'mimosa', *Acacia dealbata*, is the only wattle that you see in southern English (especially London) gardens with any frequency. Here, I was intrigued to observe that it had made a grove by dint of suckering. I hadn't realized that it could propagate from roots. However, I see that this is given as a method for certain acacias in Sheat's *Propagation of Trees, Shrubs and Conifers*.

There is a well-placed handkerchief tree, *Davidia involucrata vilmoriniana*,

Looking down the valley towards
the sea.

with wide-spreading branches, and colonies of *Viburnum plicatum* 'Lanarth',
of Cornish origin, in white bloom. I never feel secure in distinguishing this
from 'Mariesii'. Bean says: 'It [Lanarth] is really a rather coarser plant, and
certainly no more effective in the garden. It is possible that some plants grown
as "Lanarth" are really "Mariesii" and *vice versa.*'

There was one excruciatingly quarrelsome planting of two evergreen azaleas
in full bloom, one red, the other magenta. Tony Hibbert said the public
adored being photographed in front of them, so I duly made Fergus be the
public and he wore the correct, self-conscious grin.

There's a curious sense of release when you reach the unstrained dignity
of the sea shore, though rather sad that it has to be cut off from the garden by
a wall.

The return walk along the valley's west flank is largely through woodland,
the Major retailing how to set up a charitable foundation, but he was interested
in the ferns. For your chief impression, here, is of bluebells and native ferns:
common male and broad buckler; soft shield fern, lady fern, hard fern and
hart's-tongue – all there of their own accord. Beaver away at our gardens as
we may, natural woodland of this kind is hard to beat.

Three parts of the way back, you're in the garden proper again and there's a great view, slantwise across the ravine, with a cluster of three Chusan palms, *Trachycarpus fortunei*, making a key statement.

I have been writing ravine and valley alternately. Ravine is the official guide's definition, but how steeply sided a valley has to be before it can be described as a ravine, I am uncertain. I should have thought you needed some fairly sheer faces and the services of a rope or bridge to cross a ravine. The declivities at Trebah are gentle by these standards. But the garden is impressive enough and speaks for itself without verbal embellishment.

POSTSCRIPT

The Charitable Trust has gone from strength to strength. Over 70,000 visitors now come to Trebah annually and there are great plans for building a Visitor Centre and to include a lecture hall. Good news.

Why azaleas are loved and loathed.

CHAPEL KNAP

‹‹‹—◦—›››

THIS IS THE HOME of Keith and Caroline Lister and of their two children, Lucie and Chris. It feels like a home and the garden reflects a great deal of affection. Dr Lister is the chief protagonist – a mad keen plantsman, conventionally English in his love of roses and clematis, but also eccentrically English in his attraction to a huge range of plants hitherto strange to him and often having rather weird characteristics. He has to experiment with them. One result, of course, is numerous deaths, not because he is a bad gardener but because such plants (especially if they have practically no chlorophyll in their leaves) are hospital cases from the first. No harm is done if they are lost, so long as labels and any other records are quickly destroyed. Another result is that the garden is stuffed with plants either that you'd have thought too tender to survive (but nothing venture nothing win), or of whose very existence you'd not hitherto been aware.

Chapel Knap is on the Somerset coast, facing north over the Bristol Channel. The property did, indeed, run right down to the water's edge, but some was sold, before the Listers' arrival, so their egress in that direction is now confined to a right of way. There are fine views, particularly eastwards, towards Porlock. Porlock Weir is to the west. Southwards, the ground rises steeply on to Exmoor and the shadow of this hill prevents sunshine from reaching them, in winter, after mid-morning. So they are on a steep, north-facing slope and plants tend to crane their necks southwards.

But, by most of our standards, the climate is mild; mild and moist. Rainfall is 44 inches a year (with me, in East Sussex, only 30 inches). However, with light soil and free drainage, drought is often a problem and quite a bit of irrigation is laid on, especially, with trickle irrigation, in a border running parallel to the handsome red sandstone wall which divides the garden, on its south side, from a minor road.

The house, built in 1890, looks thoroughly Victorian, but its front hall includes the restored remains of a pre-Reformation Chapel of Rest (originally

thatched), dating from around 1350. A major addition by the Listers, who arrived in 1980, is a conservatory-cum-sitting-room wing, projecting eastwards, which allows of the best views through and past a couple of mature Monterey pines (*Pinus radiata*). This conservatory is as considerate to plants as to humans. There was already a pink bougainvillaea. Then a friend sent some hardwood sticks of some of the new hybrids, which 'are so spectacular, large and glaring that they compete with any plastic facsimile you might find in many an expensive store!' to quote Keith in a letter, commenting that the flowers last and last and last. *Ipomoea learii* (*I. indica*) opens a new crop of blue-purple convolvulus flowers every morning; *Dipladenia* (*Mandevilla*) *splendens* carries clusters of pink trumpets over a long season and there's a glamorous red passion flower, *Passiflora antioquiensis*. (This name might have given trouble to a lady whom the doctor was interpreting as 'spatially disorientated' when she'd had one over the odds.)

Before the Lister family's arrival, the house was owned by Captain and Mrs Christopher Leyland, who had an excellent gardener, so they inherited a number of good, mature plants. The sitting-out terrace, close to the house, is dominated by a Chusan palm, *Trachycarpus fortunei*, and there are three others of the same age. If you age this (as the horse, by the rings on its teeth) by the number of leaf scar rings on its hairy trunk, they date back to about 1890, which would fix their planting to the time the building itself went up. This palm is not to everyone's taste, but it has a presence and lends a tropical air (although, in fact remarkably hardy) which many of us would like to con ourselves into believing genuine. These palms not only flower but also self-sow, which always seems the ultimate accolade.

Another palm, native along the Mediterranean seaboard, *Chamaerops excelsa*, is also represented at Chapel Knap, making a large, shrubby boskage. It does not seed, but the fibre on its trunks is a great attraction to long-tailed tits. This is supposed to be less hardy than the trachycarpus, but I rather wonder about that. People tend to be very conservative about what they'll admit to being hardy. I think I shall give this one a try. Its scale is easier to manage (though it bulks larger) than that of trachycarpus, when once past early youth.

From Mrs Leyland's era stem two mature *Cornus capitata*, which is a species you see far more often and looking happier in the south-west than elsewhere in Britain. Its flowering, in early summer, of cream bracts is good but the crops of strawberry-like fruits that follow are even better. One of these, the child of the other, fruits much the more heavily and with larger 'berries' than its parent. Self-sown seedlings are commonplace. A snowball bush, *Viburnum plicatum*, is wedged snugly into one of the old cornuses. That sort of touch makes a garden look comfortable. There is also a fine *C. kousa chinensis*, in

The distant view of Porlock Bay. In the foreground the morning light catches the leaves of *Cornus controversa* 'Variegata' as a solitary delphinium grows through one of its tiers.

From the north terrace the view to the sea is framed by the austere trunk of a Chusan palm (*Trachycarpus fortunei*) and the green of a Monterey pine. Against this dances the lightness of the wedding-cake tree, with the strong blue spire of *Echium pininana* beyond.

bloom for many weeks in early summer, its white bracts gradually deepening, as they age, to rich pink.

To finish off the dogwoods, Keith added what he calls a wedding-cake tree, *C. controversa* 'Variegata', whose symmetrical, tabuliform growth adds another layer of horizontal branches every year. White variegation gives it an airy lightness. A nurseryman friend takes 100 shoots off it every January, for graftwood. This grows in a border extension, where it has been allowed to bulge into a diminishing lawn – sure sign of the plantsman's garden. Behind it, *Melianthus major* is now in a state of cowering suppression. I hope it will be moved; it deserves better.

To continue with my résumé of old pieces: there's a strawberry tree, *Arbutus unedo*, which is always handsome in maturity and old age, whatever shape it takes on – this one is pretty recumbent by now. The scaly trunk is reddish, the evergreen foliage cheerful. In front of it a *Crinodendron hookerianum*, a semi-tender Chilean evergreen, which can look splendid when hung with crimson lanterns; on the other hand, it can look disreputably scruffy. This one is pretty good.

There is a large Kanzan cherry – well, why not? Even if you do see it in every other suburban front garden, a mature specimen covered with double pink blossom, just about to reach its peak, is always impressive. To quote Keith: 'When the blossom falls, the wedding is over. The confetti effect on the lawn is spoilt only when you go to mow.' Autumn colour, in early November, can be brilliant. Two shrubs that keep getting larger, in old age, without achieving the gnarled dignity that we should like to imagine for ourselves, are *Carpenteria californica*, covered in white, cistus-like blossom in June, and the winter-flowering *Viburnum farreri*. But the latter gives shelter to a tender New Zealand fern, *Cyathea dealbata*, and to a variegated aspidistra!

A good Lister-generation *Viburnum plicatum* 'Pink Beauty' is another of those flowers that starts white but changes to pink on ageing. Like *Choisya ternata*, it flowers a second time in autumn. Its autumn colour is good, too.

The bed of *Paeonia lactiflora* cultivars below the sitting-out terrace is an old feature and flowers prolifically. The dreaded peony botrytis disease must have passed it by.

The moment you enter this garden, through a small gate immediately off the road, you realize that it is rich in species. *Jasminum polyanthum* grows behind *Abelia floribunda*, which is the showiest of its genus, with long tubular flowers in a daringly bright shade of carmine. The jasmine, pink in bud and opening white with a huge crop of swooningly scented blossom, manages to bring its dormant flower-buds through the winter, here. In many British gardens, it'll survive outside but fail to flower. *Brugmansia (Datura) sanguinea*, with its large burnt orange funnels, may get cut to the ground in winter (though not always), but then behaves like a herbaceous plant, flowering in late summer.

When I have enough stock of *Tetrapanax papyrifera* (it can be propagated from root cuttings), I shall risk leaving some of that outside to overwinter. Here, it appears to do so comfortably, though apt to get cut back. This is one of the best foliage plants, with large and substantial palmate leaves, hairy and fawn-coloured when young. They can be 15–18 inches (3 feet in California) across.

The sea through the deeply fissured branches of *Pinus radiata*. *Cornus kousa chinensis* makes a backcloth for old-fashioned roses.

Acacia retinoides is a wattle that is seldom out of flower, though never making much of a display.★ The florists' mimosa, *A. dealbata*, is far more dramatic in its late winter season, and its feathery foliage is delightful. Chapel Knap had a specimen higher than the house, but it was killed in a single, frosty February night in 1991. However, it comes from roots and has started up again, though at some distance from the original. That could be a little disconcerting, but at least it had the grace not to reappear through the kitchen floor.

Solanum jasminoides 'Album', so pure, fresh and long-flowering a climber, can be compared with the skimmed-milk blue type plant, much to the latter's disadvantage.† There's a Californian tree poppy, *Dendromecon rigidum*, against the house; no purer shade of yellow than that and well set off by its grey lance leaves (so un-poppylike). It has a great burst of blossom in May, followed by a sprinkling through the summer.‡ A purple-belled *Cobaea scandens* has gone berserk and survived three years.

The variegated form of *Pittosporum tobira* was struck from a cutting brought home from Jerusalem (far more exciting than buying a plant in England). The plain-leaved type plant also does well and flowers – clusters of waxy, cream white, heavily scented blossom. Keith has quite a penchant for pittosporums, most of them being located in or at the edge of a piece of woodland near the north-east corner of the house, where the garden takes a right-angular turn. There are three variegated forms of *Pittosporum tenuifolium*. Least vigorous, because shortest of chlorophyll, is 'Irene Paterson'. The leaves start white, acquiring some green colouring as they mature. 'Gauntletii' has more white variegation than 'Silver Queen' but the latter has better-shaped, incurved leaves and its black stems lend distinction. Very similar in appearance to a pittosporum and growing in the same piece of woodland is *Olearia paniculata*, with wavy-margined leaves of a bright apple green. Definitely one of the tenderer species of daisy bush. Another New Zealander, just outside the woodland area, is the semi-evergreen (it has good bronze fall colour) *Nothofagus fusca*. Only 9 inches tall when planted, it is now 35 feet tall, slim and with something of the habit of a young ginkgo, but more elegant.

Purple-leaved phormiums (more of New Zealand) look good, near by, especially when their stupendous flower spikes are silhouetted against the sea. Keith deliberately sets out to make a tropical effect, with cordylines (both *Cordyline australis* and *C. indivisa*), and *Agave americana*, which has survived several winters, though I suspect it would welcome greater exposure to sea breezes and more sunshine.

In the courtyard by the remains of the ancient chapel, on a north-facing raised bed, a kaleidoscope of leaf form and colour. *Tetrapanax papyrifera* and rodgersias contrast with *Azara microphylla* 'Variegata' and the leaves of *Hydrangea tricolor*, hostas and pulmonarias.

★ Now dead; it is difficult to keep up with the changes in a garden.
† Written before Keith 'pulled all the dirty, wishy-washy blue ones out'.
‡ This also has now died, with a list of possible replacements being contemplated.

I'm not trying to tour the garden logically, merely to point its features and plantings. Caroline comes into the picture mainly with her own, enclosed 'cottage' garden, once a traditional-type rose garden. It has a round central lawn with the borders around it. The giant *Crambe cordifolia* thrives, and many of the plants maintain themselves by self-sowing: foxgloves, moon daisies, columbines, alkanet, angelica.

Fairly newly planted with old shrub roses is an enclosed oblong garden on the next terrace below this. The hedges are interesting. Lots of shelter is needed (as in most British gardens). *Elaeagnus × ebbingei* runs along one side; a coarse evergreen, but efficient and deliciously scented when flowering in autumn. On the opposite, down side, the bright green *Griselinia littoralis*, with soap-smooth foliage, is as cheerful in winter as in any season. Excellent near the sea. Mixed in is a good deal of *Myrtus luma* (*Luma apiculata*), a Chilean species, generous with its white blossom and managing to flower pretty well despite clipping.

From Caroline's cottage garden, Hurlestone Point across the bay is wreathed by the confetti-like *Crambe cordifolia*. Marguerites (*Argyranthemum frutescens*), always in flower, thrive in the light soil and the sun. *Iris sibirica* in the near foreground and the purple-leaved sage accentuate the overall feeling of lightness.

Downhill, the vegetables, including magnificent globe artichokes, and finally the grass tennis court. This is a most important feature, as Chris (in his early teens by now) is a promising player, who goes in for plenty of competitions.

So far I have missed much of the garden on the upper levels. There are several terraced, compartmented areas adjacent to the roadside wall. Although facing north, the border under this is not overhung by trees so it receives a good deal of light. The climbing *Lapageria rosea*, with its pendent, waxy pink bells, does well. That doesn't relish a hot position, anyway. The white form of *Crinum × powellii* is free with its amaryllis-like display and that is a greater surprise.

With the help of the trickle irrigation, hostas and ferns are lush; the coarsely show-off *Hosta* 'Frances Williams', with its broad yellowish margin to a muscular, glaucous leaf, is well partnered by a self-sown male fern. And there is a glaucous hosta to contrast with the varyingly bronzed foliage of *Heuchera* 'Palace Purple' seedlings. These are in the Pool Garden, a formal pool and the area where Chris sets up his tent when sleeping out in summer. The summerhouse at the far end of this garden has polypody ferns (self-appointed, of course) growing on its thatched roof. A widely spaced structure around this garden's perimeter on its north and east sides has been planted with climbing roses, leaving gaps between the uprights for the view towards Porlock.

I have probably under-emphasized the part played by roses in this garden. Old, once-flowering kinds like 'Céleste', 'Raubritter' and 'Königin von Dänemark' will keep the addict for the old shrub types happy, in June, while I was attracted, seeing it at just its right moment, by a once-flowering modern shrub type, ridiculously named 'Pink Bells'. About 6 feet tall (it is marketed as ground cover, that magic formula), it carried very pretty, smallish double pink blossom on a bush that is ready to cascade if perched aloft a little. Blue love-in-a-mist (*Nigella damascena*) seeds in the path below year after year. Keith also describes 'under the "Pink Bells", masses of wild buttercups – yellow with pink – wonderful'.

On the roadside wall there is a double yellow Banksian rose, which used to be supported by a Judas tree, *Cercis siliquastrum*. Its flowers are brilliant pink with a dash of mauve. The two together must have looked smashing, in May, but the Judas tree collapsed (one can hardly blame it) and had to be removed.

As I remarked, the doctor can't resist a freak. There was a 15-inch-tall rose bush that had just enough life in it to carry a few double yellow blooms with a bronze-red basal zone (reminding me of a halimiocistus) at the base of each petal. Another, equally feeble, has white-variegated foliage; I think he called it 'Pink Break'. Of *Stranvaesia* (now *Photinia*) *davidiana* 'Palette', the one with pink and white variegation, 'It never looks very well,' Dr Lister commented, understandingly. 'I'm not a eucalyptus man,' said he, as we passed a scrubby example which he maybe inherited. 'I can see that,' I agreed.

But the garden overflows with voluptuously complacent plants. The doctor has gone in for bark mulches in a big way, of recent years. They retain moisture and contribute nitrogen in the long run, especially if composted well before application (which looks a lot better, too). The supply comes from Wales. Despite the mulches, many plants self-sow, as I have already indicated. The now ubiquitous *Lavatera* 'Barnsley' is a prolific mother, and one of the offspring was white all through. The tree mallows *Abutilon vitifolium* and the deeper mauve, though smaller-flowered *A. ochsenii* are constantly self-sowing and intercrossing. You never know what will turn up. It is the same with agapanthus.

More boldly exotic-looking plants include *Beschorneria yuccoides*, which does indeed have yucca-like leaves, though glaucous. It has already, at quite an early age, thrown up its thrilling inflorescence (in May) of large pink bracts and small green and purple bells. *Echium pininana* (see my Isle of Wight chapter, page 8), with its giant rosettes of hairy grey foliage, was looking well behind an excellent narrow-leaved bush of a *Calceolaria integrifolia* cultivar, covered with small, bright yellow blossom. Another good combination, in a sunny spot, had the white daisies (against lacy grey foliage) of *Anthemis cupaniana* next to the rich red-purple daisies of *Osteospermum* 'Tresco Purple'. A part of the rapidly increasing National Osteospermum Collection is held here. So it will be appreciated that Keith's tastes are very catholic.

He has a good range of hydrangeas, including long flowerers like *Hydrangea arborescens*, the white hortensia 'Mme Émile Mouillère', and the small bun-headed 'Preziosa', which starts pale pink and gradually intensifies to ruby red. Also a good red lacecap, called 'Happiness', so the doctor told me, given him by his wife on their fifth wedding anniversary. I couldn't find any reference to this in my books. Caroline, on being referred back to, thought its name was actually 'Endurance'. I can't find that either. A name change every few years wouldn't be surprising.

Wales, Northern England, Scotland and Ireland

POWIS CASTLE

POWIS CASTLE is one of the few National Trust properties that I have chosen to write about here. The reasons for leaving most of them out are first that the NT has been lavish in self-advertisement, there being entire books devoted to their gardens alone; even more cogent, that their properties, having lost the living core of an owning family, are institutionalized and faceless, being run by committees. This is not levelled as a criticism. It is inevitable and we are duly grateful to the NT for preserving properties that would probably otherwise have met with a disastrous fate.

In a few cases, however, certain gardens have risen above the usual homogenized image because of the presence of a hands-on head gardener who, over a period of twenty years, perhaps, or more, has stamped his (or her, of course) image and expertise on what has become his handiwork. He may often be maddened by officialdom (which is, I grant, supportive also), but becomes so devoted to what has become, to an extent, his garden, that he will not tear himself away from it until forced to by retirement. (Lucky the owner-occupier who never needs to retire.)

Powis Castle has had Jimmy Hancock in charge since 1972. Well done, Powis Castle. Everywhere you look has the stamp of expertise and imagination (some of it provided by Graham Thomas). It is an exciting garden, its varied selection of plants always truly well grown and well presented.

To state a few basics. The property, close to the small town of Welshpool, is just over the Welsh border from Shropshire. Annual rainfall is 32 inches, not much exceeding what my garden receives in East Sussex. The soil is heavy and water-retaining, fertile (with help) and good if you know how to handle it. The pH is slightly above neutral, by and large, so the nineteenth-century craze for rhododendron planting barely affected Powis. A more recently acquired adjacent site, of ten and a half acres, has acid soil and does allow rhododendrons and other calcifuge plants to be included. The castle, standing on an eminence above the terraced gardens, was built in the twelfth and

An ornamental pot spilling over with fuchsias and *Diascia rigescens*.

thirteenth centuries with red sandstone quarried from areas that are now garden. It became NT property in 1952 and there are now some 100,000 visitors per annum. Quite a success story. There are eight gardeners.

The garden's framework, besides terrace walling, consists mainly of yew and box hedging and topiary. The yew topiary is massive, even grotesque, and doubtless quite different from what was originally contemplated when first planted, but this suits the locale. After all, the castle itself is pretty heavy and looks all the better for the support of blocky vegetation.

Some of the box is of a vigorous variety and reaches a height more often considered suitable for yew. Jimmy pointed out to me that box hedging always grows more densely and satisfactorily on its sunny face. The shaded side will inevitably be threadbare by comparison. This will be noticed, especially, where double borders, fronted by box hedging, run east and west, as here. Jimmy has found that short-bladed mechanical hedge-trimmers (Little Wonder is the make he favours) do a better controlled job than long, 30-inch blades, especially

The castle and terraces with vast, overgrown yews.

where you are trimming an undulating surface. If the blades start sharp and are set correctly, they should be self-sharpening. Attempts to sharpen them yourself can do more damage than good.

The flower borders on each terrace have their own distinctive character. At the upper level they largely comprise the tender perennials that Jimmy manages so well. Why are more gardeners not using them? Certainly you need the back-up of glass, but most British gardeners have some of that and, in many instances, heating can be kept to an inexpensive minimum.

Jimmy is particularly good with salvias. The deep blue *Salvia patens*, the light sky blue, white-flecked *S. uliginosa*, more than 6 feet tall and making an impressive back-of-border colony; that is pretty hardy. *S. confertiflora*, with large leaves crowned by spikes of small, deep red flowers, is not. Most impressive and desirable is the shrubby *S. leucantha*. That has grey, felted leaves, a silvery inflorescence in which the corolla itself is rich lavender blue. Quite apart from its not being hardy, the snag with this sage is that it tends to start flowering so late in the season (in our climate, that is) as to give us little value before autumnal frosts intervene.

Jimmy puts out large plants, hardened off from glasshouse protection, and he believes in getting them out as early as April. They were already coming into flower on 2 August, when I was last there, so the success of his method speaks for itself.

I will detail other flowers in this excitingly lush area before going on to foliage, which by its size, swagger and longevity contributes most to a border or garden to which you wish to give a subtropical flavour. *Rehmannia elata* (better known as *R. angulata*) was considered till recently to be a conservatory plant only, but its hardiness is well worth testing outside and it is easily raised from seed. It has loose racemes of open-mouthed, rosy lilac bells on a 2-foot plant. I think this was my first sighting of *Nicotiana glauca*, a truly tender perennial which one keeps going from cuttings. Its habit tends to be tall and little branching with wonderfully glaucous leaves (quite small and neat) and small, tubular green flowers. Its chief asset is in looking different. *N. sylvestris* we should all know and grow by now: large, bright green paddle leaves supporting a magnificent candelabrum of white flowers, their long tubes opening to smallish limbs at the mouth. This has a creamy scent. The plant makes 6 feet or more of height if started early.

Various daisy flowers such as *Osteospermum* 'Whirligig', blue and white with crimped rays; *Argyranthemum* 'Jamaica Primrose'; a cream-coloured everlasting, new to me, *Helichrysum* 'Sky Net'. *Geranium palmatum* carries its brash pink flowers above bold palmate leaves for a long time and, although short-lived, self-sows, being pretty hardy, much more so than *G. maderense*, with which it

A border with tender perennials adjoining Jimmy Hancock's house.

is so often confused. The summer-flowering, lime-tolerant *Erica terminalis*, a sizeable 'tree' heath, was a bit of a surprise in such company, but why not? Penstemons were there, and some of the colourful but tender hebes like crimson 'Simon Delaux' and purple 'La Séduisante'. Theirs is a long flowering season, especially if you keep up with dead-heading.

A striking group that I photographed had *Fuchsia* 'Gartenmeister Bonstedt', *Calceolaria* 'Kentish Hero' and the loose, grey, pinnate-leaved *Artemisia arborescens* together. The calceolaria is bronze-coloured; so are the undersides of the fuchsia's leaves, while its long, tubular flowers are little short of scarlet and very showy. It is widely represented at Powis, especially in pots and other containers.

The suckering shrub *Clerodendrum bungei* has bold, dark heart leaves as well as terminal domes of deep pink, sweetly scented flowers late summer to autumn. The curving pink inflorescence of *Canna iridiflora* is charming, but its banana-like green foliage (with a narrow purple rim) is really its dominant feature. It is hardy enough to be left out, being given a covering of dead leaves.

Foliage, then, includes the indispensable *Melianthus major*, with large, glaucous leaves, boldly toothed at their margins. This South African is hardy once established. I protect its crown and cut it to the ground in spring, even if old growth has survived. Young shoots make the lushest display. *Nandina domestica*, a smallish shrub with compound pinnate leaves, copper when young, makes a good showing here. It can be a bit scrawny, but benefits from feeding and occasional hardish pruning. The cream- and the white-variegated *Aralia elata* have huge pinnate leaves. They need to be grafted and are expensive. If their roots are damaged, they sucker back to the green-leaved stock. Sword leaves are represented by New Zealand flax, *Phormium tenax* (you have to allow for a height of 7 feet), yuccas and the yucca-like *Cordyline australis*.

Down two levels, the terrace is wide enough to accommodate double herbaceous borders in two sections. One of them, the westernmost, has soft, pastel shades while the easterly concentrates on hot colours: red, orange, yellow, purple and white (which is certainly a strong colour). Aspect makes a difference to the way you should plant, especially in east–west borders, where the flowers are viewed either from the south or from the north. It is silly slavishly to replicate your plantings in the two borders. Many flowers, especially daisies (sunflowers are the prototypes, 'counting the steps of the sun', as Blake had it), face mainly southwards (northwards in the southern hemisphere). If planted in the south border, you'll have only the backs of the flowers to look at. Even foxgloves tend to concentrate their blossom on the sunny side of the spike. That is a graceful arrangement so long as you are correctly placed for viewing it.

So in the hot borders crocosmias are an obvious choice, and do well on the heavy soil. Jimmy was shocked by their wretched performance in the Wisley trials, as I was also. When short of water and overheated, they can easily be killed by red spider mites. Jimmy makes a habit, as do I, of lifting and splitting cultivars of *Anthemis tinctoria*, with their cream or yellow daisies, every year, this being done in autumn. Spare material is kept in reserve. In this way you get a much longer flowering from the rejuvenated plants, which are also shorter-stemmed and more easily managed. Another plant he lifts, splits and resets annually, for similar reasons, is *Sedum* 'Autumn Joy'. Left to itself, it grows too tall and the group splays outwards under its own excessive weight, leaving an unsightly open centre.

He likes frequent splitting of a good deal of herbaceous stuff. *Sisyrinchium striatum* keeps on flowering, if rejuvenated, and does not give that unsavoury yet characteristic display of blackened old foliage. All the strains of shasta daisy benefit from frequent division. I like one, here, called 'Aglaia', no more than 3 feet tall, semi-double and with divided ends to its dead white rays. *Chrysanthemum maximum* is now *Leucanthemum* × *superbum*.

Although it had finished flowering by August, I was impressed by the size of *Hedysarum coronarium*, which had made a 4-foot, wide-spreading bush, each branchlet terminated, in its season, by a dense spike of red pea flowers. You grow this from seed and plants usually last a couple of years.

Dahlias here and elsewhere remain *in situ* for many years. The purple 'Admiral Rawnsley' had done at least fifteen and makes a height of 10 feet.

The tendency, nowadays, is to favour a shorter plant, so it is no surprise that this variety has dropped out of the catalogues, but tall dahlias can have their uses. Their staking has to be efficient! These, also located in the autumn border on the next level down, are covered with magnolia leaves in winter. Clematis were here represented at the back by rich purple 'Royal Velours' and the double old-rose 'Purpurea Plena Elegans'.

The cool-coloured double borders had the unsurpassable clematis 'Perle d'Azur' against the terrace wall. I photographed it with *Romneya coulteri*, its large white flowers having yellow stamens and a backing of glaucous foliage; and *Argyranthemum* 'Vancouver', which is a double, anemone-centred pink daisy. Another clematis flowering freely in this section (it often doesn't) was 'Huldine', with moderate-sized white flowers, pearly mauve on the underside. Clematis here and elsewhere are trained on Jackman Hoops, of solid iron and dating back to Edwardian times, when these borders were already extant.

I was taken by a quite small-flowered, lemon yellow perennial sunflower, which I gather is called 'Lemon Queen'. It also features in the Cottage Garden at Sissinghurst Castle.

On the narrower terrace, next down, the borders are one-sided, one for autumn, one for May–June. There are some unusual wall plants at Powis Castle. The Cape figwort, *Phygelius capensis*, does far better like this, reaching a height of 12 feet, than as a free-standing shrub. So, as I have seen it similarly treated at the High Beeches in Sussex, does *Phygelius aequalis* 'Yellow Trumpet'. In a border, it is far too leafy. While on the subject, another good way to grow them is in the cracks of dry walling. They love the free drainage and somewhat starved conditions. *Malva sylvestris* 'Primley Blue', a strikingly blue mallow normally seen as a prostrate plant, displays itself with great panache at Powis, where it makes a height of 7 feet.

Below the terrace we have reached is a steep, grassy bank, gay in spring and early summer with primroses, daffodils and ox-eyed daisies. All this is cut in July and there follows a display of colchicums. Below this bank is the great lawn, though it had fountains and statuary in the late eighteenth century.

At the top end of the lawn, on the right as you look down from the terraces, is a rather boggy area (below a big pond) which is most interestingly planted, with suckering shrubs and tough perennials such as will cope with rough grass. The Germans practise this system in many of their Garden Festival sites. Some shrubs included here were the white-stemmed bramble, *Rubus cockburnianus*; red-stemmed dogwood, *Cornus alba*; sorbaria, with creamy white terminal panicles of spiraea-like flowers; and willow. All these actually benefit from being regularly cut hard back. Then the perennials, many of them

In the lower garden, *Clematis × jackmanii* behind pale hollyhocks; the shrubby *Malva alcea fastigiata* and the annual *Venidium fastuosum* 'Zulu Prince' at the margin.

too embarrassingly large or coarse for inclusion in polite garden compartments. Giant *Gunnera manicata*, as expected, and I think of the water saxifrage, *Damera peltata*, on the same wavelength, its smaller leaves also peltate (umbrella-like). *Inula magnifica* is a giant yellow daisy that I do find room for in my principal mixed border (being a sucker for yellow daisies). The green-centred cone flower, *Rudbeckia* 'Herbstsonne' ('Autumn Sun') is just about as tall but flops hopelessly in a border, whereas it often remains upright in an open situation and anyway a semi-collapsed condition may not look out of place if the setting is wild and prairie-like.

Cicerbita (Lactuca) plumieri is a handsome tall perennial, if not quite trained to boudoir manners, with panicles of blue-purple blossom. It is a composite with ligulate rays. *Eupatorium purpureum*, Joe Pie weed to the Americans and clearly big brother to our hemp agrimony, *E. cannabinum*, obviously belongs to this company, with corymbs of fuzzy purple blossom in late summer. Loosestrifes, both purple (*Lythrum*) and yellow (*Lysimachia punctata* and *L. ciliata*, both with running rootstocks), were well represented. Then, at the top pond level, a magnificent stand, in the partial shade of trees, of *Acanthus spinosus*. I should love to establish that in a rough place and am currently

Tapestry planting against the stairway ramp with *Euonymus × fortunei* 'Silver Queen' against the wall: santolinas, zauschnerias, *Verbena* 'Silver Anne', *Ceratostigma willmottianum* in front.

making the attempt. As every piece of damaged root makes a new plant, Hydra-like, it is a bit of a liability in mixed border conditions.

Now I must turn to the flat area on the other side of the lower garden, where there were once fruit trees and vegetables. An effective feature is made by a vine pergola. At the base of each vine, on its post, is a square cut out from lawn and planted with golden marjoram, kept neat and clipped. Most effective at a distance and the marjoram does not appear to scorch, which I find its vicious habit during hot, dry spells in my garden. Another unusual feature is of *Lonicera × americana* grown as standards in a row, with square underplantings, alternately, of the near black *Ophiopogon planiscapus* 'Nigrescens' and of a variegated pale yellow and green carex (sedge).

I can pick out only a selection of plants and plantings that struck me. Along a low wall on one side of this area is a continuous, luminous band of the bright yellow ivy, *Hedera colchica* 'Dentata Aurea', again not a bit scorched, although fully exposed to sunshine. The heavy, moisture-retaining soil must be a help in this respect.

There is a richly planted border against a higher wall on the other side of this garden, including diascias (the bold *Diascia rigescens*, prominent, but I do tire of the mawkish salmon pink colouring that diascias specialize in) and argyranthemums, bedded out. One splendid grouping had a purple Jackman clematis on the wall, then pale yellow hollyhocks and in front of them a bush of the pink, hollyhock-related *Malva alcea fastigiata*. At the border front, a pastel-shaded yarrow (one of the recent *Achillea millefolium* hybrids out of Germany) and *Venidium fastuosum* 'Zulu Prince', an irresistible annual South

African daisy, white with a black disc and dotted rings around the centre, of black and orange. It flowers all summer. This is a mixture of permanent, semi-permanent and ephemeral ingredients offering scope for endless permutations. Never any need to become set and stale.

The hollyhocks looked exceptionally healthy and inquiry revealed that Jimmy sprays them against rust disease betimes and *before* signs of trouble appear. Other mallows, like 'Primley Blue', require the same protection.

What I would call tapestry plantings are very much in Jimmy's line. Where a flight of steps descends by a stone-capped ramp (with a covered urn making a finial at the end) from one terrace to the next, the border planting in front of it is so well integrated, dignified and simple, yet interesting, too, as to make you catch your breath. Against the diagonal wall ramp itself grows the lively green and cream *Euonymus × fortunei* 'Silver Queen', which becomes a self-clinging climber as soon as it feels a solid surface behind it. In the border, domes of clipped lavender cotton, *Santolina chamaecyparissus* and *S. pinnata neapolitana*, with another santolina dome, as yet unpruned and thus covered with buttons of pale, creamy yellow blossom (not the brash, unwelcome yellow of the first two, when allowed to bloom). Mixed in, the blue plumbago flower-heads of *Ceratostigma willmottianum* and the bright red funnels of zauschneria. Another weaver, here, the bedding verbena (not infrequently capable of overwintering) with heads of pink, scented blossom, 'Silver Anne'. Thus you have a number of solid, principal ingredients and then the infillers. No soil, no wall in sight.

One of the liveliest border plantings is in front of Jimmy's own dwelling, to one side of the main garden but very much a part of it. Here there is a high, backing wall on which a white-flowered clone of everlasting pea, *Lathyrus latifolius*, and the equally pure white *Solanum jasminoides* 'Album' were flowering in August, while blood red 'Bishop of Llandaff' dahlias were in exciting contrast, in front. There were orange arctotis, red-and-white penstemons, white, glaucous-leaved *Argyranthemum foeniculaceum* – altogether a lot of blossom, grouped yet unregimented.

A final paragraph should be devoted to the many ornamental pots, urns, troughs and other containers, which are such a feature at Powis Castle and in whose summer planting Jimmy Hancock excels. Their contents include all the sort of ingredients that you would expect – *Helichrysum petiolare* cultivars, fuchsias, pelargoniums, lobelias (the spraying blue *Lobelia richardsonii*, which you keep going from cuttings, among them), and diascias. Everything so cultivated as to provide an abundance of blossom and growth. You almost take these things for granted, when they just seem to have happened, but there is much behind-the-scenes skill involved. This is a garden worth revisiting.

BELSAY HALL

———⊰•⊱———

THE GARDENS at Belsay Hall are among the most romantic I know. Romance in this context depends in part on a sense of mystery, of faded historical association and an element of neglect. Once you introduce hordes of public, necessitating hard paths, easy gradients for wheeled chairs, notices, directional arrows, loos, refreshment facilities, car-parking and other marks of civilization, something of the romance will be lost. There is no help for this. Properties cannot survive indefinitely on neglect. We must be, and are, grateful when they come under the care of a responsible organization, as, in this case, of English Heritage.

But only some 15,000 people were, through the year, visiting Belsay when I first came to it on a sombre September day, with scarcely a soul in sight. Situated fifteen miles north-west of Newcastle upon Tyne, in North-umberland, the feel of the area is strongly North Country, unsmiling, a little grim, but genuine.

Belsay Hall, a ponderous neo-classical pile, was built in the early years of the nineteenth century and is divorced by the whole length of its garden from the original castle, dating from around 1370. It was in the Middleton family for all that time and until a few years ago, when the late Sir Stephen made it over to English Heritage.

It is mainly to the vision of Sir Charles that we owe the gardens that he created (when building the Hall) and subsequently developed, for he lived till 1867. Sir Charles Monck, as he had to become in order to inherit property on his mother's side of the family, built Belsay Hall from stone quarried next to it. The quarrying was done in such a way as to create the framework for a quarry garden, with cliff faces, stone archways, bluffs and islands of rock left standing after what was needed for the Hall had been removed. He was passionate about plants and tried out many that had only recently been introduced to Britain from exotic habitats. The surprising presence of a Chusan palm, *Trachycarpus fortunei*, in the quarry, was one of these intro-

Belsay Hall from the south-east, overlooking the rhododendron garden begun in the 1860s and planted largely with hardy hybrid rhododendrons between 1903 and 1933.

ductions. Sir Charles was followed, in 1867, by his grandson Arthur, who reverted to the name of Middleton. He was an equally enthusiastic gardener, living till 1933 and responsible, during the 1920s, for much of the rhododendron plantings.

From 1860 on, these two made the rhododendron garden, which lies to the south of the Hall and is not yet open to the public. Most rhododendron woods used to be planted with selected varieties grafted on *Rhododendron ponticum* stock. This is the ubiquitous species that has taken over large areas of acid soil in England and Scotland. Its bright mauve flowers can, in June, make a wonderful landscape impression, when softened by distance, but when the stock suckers, which it does, eventually, in most cases, it takes over from the original cultivar that was intended, and the plantings revert to *ponticum* alone. Not so at Belsay, where the owners were keen to have their rhododendrons on their own roots (achieved, in those days, by layering). Old trees of such as the raw pink 'Cynthia', the purple-blotched 'Sappho' and the magnificent late double mauve 'Fastuosum Plenum', are still present (so, even, are some of the original labels) and healthy. You walk among their rugged trunks with a canopy of blossom above your head and a carpet of spent blooms beneath your soles.

In the centre of this garden is a vast Scotch laburnum, *Laburnum alpinum*, hung with its short racemes of scented, yellow blossom in early summer and remarkably at home in the company of so much pink and mauve. This laburnum has a diameter of 35 yards (I paced it). I presume it to be over a century old and it has a method of self-perpetuation that lasts indefinitely. A cluster of trunks arises from a stool. As these age, they splay outwards, under their own weight, eventually lying along the ground and, later still, rotting, but new branches have meantime arisen from the prostrate trunk. There is another equally impressive specimen where the public can enjoy it, along the route to the castle and not far short of it. Laburnums do like the north.

The rhododendron garden also includes, on the side nearest to and viewed from the Hall, deciduous azalea plantings, notably Ghent hybrids, which make large bushes covered with small blossom and have a far more relaxed and less aggressive appearance than the larger Mollis and Exbury hybrids, which superseded them in popularity.

Big features in this garden which stand out as seen from a distance include Lawson's cypress, yew and birch. Tucked away, there is a badger's sett — another reason, perhaps, for not opening the area up.

The big laburnum in the rhododendron garden can now be seen by the public from the new, one-and-a-half-mile walk down beside the rhododendrons to the lake and around the Crag wood behind. 'The views back,' writes Stephen Anderton, 'are terrific, and you see the Hall rising, like a Wurlitzer organ in a cinema, from the flaming rhododendrons!'

My first visit to Belsay was before it took on Stephen Anderton as head gardener. He has made a tremendous difference to all standards of upkeep, renovations and new plantings. Visitors per annum were up to 70,000 at my last inquiry, and still rising. Stephen, who now oversees some three North of England gardens for English Heritage and gives advice on others, trained for drama in Birmingham, when a younger man. He has many interests, including music and the composition of songs; he has marked vaudeville leanings. But he is a Yorkshireman and disinclined to show emotion unless wound up. Stephen is a friend (he dislikes adjectives). He is also one of the best half-dozen writers on gardening in this country. Perhaps that doesn't say quite as much as it sounds, because few genuine gardeners feel comfortable when trying to express themselves on paper.

Before he arrived, the extensive terraces below the house had been planted up to plans by Elizabeth Banks, for English Heritage. There were already good pieces worth preserving, notably some *Pieris floribunda*, reckoned to be eighty or ninety years old. Also *Magnolia × thompsoniana* (a cross between the highly scented, summer-flowering *M. tripetala* and *M. virginiana*). It makes a large, ungainly shrub, flowering from June onwards.

The pair of enormous central beds rise, like a wedding cake, in two tiers and were doubtless bedded out in their Victorian heyday. They comprise mixed shrub and herbaceous plantings, now, offering good skyline silhouettes with that incomparable grass, *Stipa gigantea*, giant fennel, agapanthus heads and others. The season is prolonged. Autumn colour includes yellow daisies of various persuasions, *Hypericum* 'Hidcote', pink border phloxes, the carpet-making *Persicaria affine* 'Superba', whose long-lasting pokers change gradually from pasty pink to deep ruby; the white shepherd's crook *Lysimachia clethroides*; *Monarda* 'Beauty of Cobham', with whorls of pink flowers set off by purple bracts; *Fuchsia* 'Tom Thumb', which looks rather surprised to find itself rubbing cheeks with *Acanthus spinosus*. And St Dabeoc's heath, *Daboecia cantabrica*, remains, with its large pinky mauve bells, in flower for several months.

There are also good foliage effects, with the grey-leaved sun rose, *Helianthemum* 'Wisley Pink', slaty *Hebe recurva*, the deckle-edged, shiny leaves of mat-forming *Dryas octopetala*, Jackman's blue rue, wispy stems of *Cytisus praecox*. The comfrey, *Symphytum × uplandicum* 'Variegatum', its big oval leaves broadly margined in cream, always makes its boldest showing on the second foliage flush that follows cutting down its flowering stems around midsummer. Yuccas suit this kind of garden and Stephen has planted a number of them. A pattern of large beds at ground level (most everything is on a large scale) make a mainly summer display with the dark-leaved *Hebe* 'Mrs Winder' (replacing 'Hidcote' lavender), *Alchemilla mollis*, 'Laced Joy' pinks and scented hybrid musk roses 'Felicia' and 'Moonlight', the latter having rich purple young foliage but white flowers. Both these are repeat-flowering, when the short Northumbrian growing season allows.

You move westwards into a small rectangular garden that Sir Arthur Middleton enclosed with hedges to make of it a 'flower garden', subsequently a rose garden. The hedges are greedy. It was not a success but Stephen thinks he has made it so – without roses but to include topiary pieces (more hungry roots, but then he appreciates the importance of feeding). A *Hosta plantaginea* hybrid was hopeless, here, as its flowering (which is important) is too late to make it, in this cool climate. The area is now bedded out and, in its summer season, works well.

There follows the magnolia terrace, with a big cucumber tree, *Magnolia acuminata*. Flowers are of little account but the cucumber-shaped fruits should be a talking point (here, their diminutive size is a bit pathetic) and the large, deciduous leaves are impressive, colouring well in autumn. There are also nice mounds of Portugal laurel, *Prunus lusitanica*, which have grown into prosperous mounds following a hard cut back.

Rather to my surprise, *Hydrangea* 'Preziosa' thrives in a south-facing bed running alongside the path. It is one of my favourites but I shouldn't have expected it to be hardy, here. The small bun-headed flower-heads change from pale to dark in the manner just described of *Persicaria affine* 'Superba', but its leaf petioles are also dark red.

A big old holly hedge divides this garden from the Winter Garden, where heathers are the principal theme, and a great success they are. The low, carpeting kinds can lap over the path's marginal stone coping without being trodden on, as the gravel path is 9 feet wide. Other low shrubs associate well with these heathers, providing firmer foliage; notably *Daphne retusa* and the creeping *Mahonia nervosa*, which I have failed to please in my garden. It comes from Oregon, on the Pacific coast, and has a most stylish leaf. I also liked *Berberis calliantha*, a low ground-covering evergreen species, grey on the leaf undersides, glossy green on top and carrying pale yellow blossom in spring.

Heathers, tree heaths and azaleas in the Winter Garden. To the rear is a Douglas fir, planted from the original introduction in 1827. The large tree heaths, *Erica arborea* 'Alpina', date from *c*. 1910 and have been cut to the ground regularly throughout their lives.

Ferns and an interweaving carpet of *Claytonia sibirica*.

The quarry at its narrowest, overhung with trees. Gardening here is with moss and wood sorrel, ferns, and light and shade only. The arch and doorway are late nineteenth-century.

Variation in height is largely provided by tree heaths, *Erica lusitanica* and *E. arborea alpina*, the former having particularly fresh, light green foliage at every season. What of their hardiness? you might well inquire. Not at all too bad. Weight of snow is a greater hazard than cold. They had been slashed hard back, shortly before I first saw them, to make them stock out and have responded extremely well from the old stumps.

There are also bigger, background shrubs. Of *Picea abies* 'Clanbrassiliana', which is a chunky shrub form of the Norwegian spruce, Stephen remarked that snow on its shoot tips was held like a pie crust. There are two of these.

At one end of the Winter Garden is a large rectangle of mown grass which used to be a pair of tennis courts, but was just unused lawn when Stephen arrived on the scene. It was his idea and enterprise to convert them into two croquet lawns, and they are now much used by Belsay Hall's own croquet club. A high wall on the far (south) side is clothed in vines (*Vitis coignetiae, V. vinifera* and a Virginia creeper, *Parthenocissus henryana*), while on the low walls on the path side are the evergreen *Cotoneaster microphyllus* with Cape figwort, *Phygelius capensis* 'African Queen'.

A door in the far corner of this garden leads you across a farm road and into a woodland alley, where snowdrops, bluebells, martagon lilies, forms of meadow cranesbill (*Geranium pratense*), *Claytonia* (*Montia*) *sibirica* making sheets of white in early summer and *Saxifraga × geum* likewise, ending with colchicums, effectively cover the growing season at the field layer. There is also a 6-foot high hedge of the evergreen *Gaultheria shallon*, one of the keenest entrants for the hotly contested honour of dullest ground-cover shrub. To be fair (if I must), it does have a shiny, light-reflecting leaf. There is a big colony of the mildly invasive *Persicaria campanulata* – just right for this kind of situation and providing a long, late display of its small, pale pink bells. Behind this, a large specimen of *Rosa moyesii*, laden with red hips in their season.

Next into the Meadow Garden. The turf is coarse but includes cowslips, an experimental planting of snakeshead fritillaries, a range of *Geranium pratense* forms, *G. sylvestris* and its albino. *Camassia quamash*, the North American bulb with spikes of star-shaped, deep blue flowers in May, has also established well. Then, after its annual cut, colchicums. There are large, spreading specimens of *Parrotia persica*, purchased in 1911 at 11s. 6d. each. That is particularly noted for its autumn colour. Big, billowing trees of the conifer which covers so much of Japan, *Cryptomeria japonica*, its branches making voluptuous, open sprays.

And so into the quarry. This is divided into two sections by an arch and it is crowned and overhung by yews and pines, planted above the rock walls. They make both a screen and a presence. A Chilean conifer, *Fitzroya cup-*

ressoides, dated from William Lobb's first collection of this species for Veitch's nursery, in 1849. Greater spotted woodpeckers had nested in it. A gale has recently blown it away, and a youngster is in its place. There are fine specimens of rhododendron species and early hybrids dating from plantings early in this century, and a very big *Eucryphia glutinosa*, the best of its genus, in my opinion, not only for its white blossoms, with their wealth of red-tipped stamens, but for its late fall colour, this being a deciduous species.

The sheltered situation suits large-leaved rhododendrons and I noted a recently planted *R. sino-grande* with leaves 18 inches long. But although the atmosphere is moist, the freely draining, sandy rubble can become very dry and this sometimes creates problems for the plants in a bog garden, here. (I couldn't see any problems myself, but Stephen assured me of them.) Ferns revel everywhere, including the royal fern, *Osmunda regalis*, which seems to

The Quarry Garden pond and Great Arch beyond. Stone from the quarry was used for the building of the Hall and the new village in the early nineteenth century. Ferns, gunnera and irises make a strong contrast with the bold rocks. Winter-flowering species rhododendrons grow on the quarry floor, with *Rhododendron ponticum* tumbling over the cliff tops.

belong to the same class as *Gunnera manicata*. That loves it here. There was even too much of the running shuttlecock fern, *Matteuccia struthiopteris* (it has now been called to order), though its fronds remain fresh throughout the growing season. In the south they are only too liable to scorch. There are also colourful plantings of bog irises and primulas. On a sunny day in June, the quarry can even wear a smiling aspect.

But it is more like itself under lowering skies. From my first, autumn, visit, I especially remember the huge curtains of growth hanging over large islands of rock at the quarry's far end, consisting of an ivy and a *Vitis coignetiae*, which is the vine with the largest leaves. They can colour dazzlingly, in autumn, but seldom do on this specimen.

A second archway closes the quarry and you emerge into a treed walk with a fine laburnum and a huge specimen of the Italian alder, *Alnus cordata*. I should love to see that flowering, in April. And so to the old castle. There is a meadow, here, rich in *Erythronium dens-canis*, so I am told, but the romance of the garden now lies behind us.

I have not mentioned the monkey puzzles, *Araucaria araucana*, of which there are, I think, four surviving specimens. Anyway, they include male and female trees (it is wise to stand clear when cones are falling off the latter) and home-grown seedlings have been raised, fifteen of them now planted out. Growth in the early years is slow. Worth waiting for, though, and they are just the sort of trees to suit a Victorian garden such as this.

With luck (and enough cash), there should be some good years ahead for it. There is no doubt that Stephen loves the place, even the dry-rot-scarred shell of the Hall, which is more than I do. But the gardens are another matter. They deserve to be worked for *con amore*.

BALCARRES

———⊱•⊰———

BALCARRES is in Fife. The Bass Rock, in the Firth of Forth, can be seen in the distance. So this is, basically, a maritime climate but, being on the east coast, rainfall is low. In Scotland that doesn't count for so much as does the relatively cool climate, so that plants generally considered as shade-loving are just as happy growing in the sun and rubbing cheeks with accepted sun-lovers.

All this and much more has been discovered and made use of by Ruth Crawford, the Countess of Crawford and Balcarres, who is one of the most adventurous and creative gardeners I have ever met. She never goes into the garden to show you round without a notebook; she is always taking on new ideas and experimenting with them and the results speak for themselves. They are exciting, stimulating and, much of the time, successful.

This is a large garden (don't ask me how many acres), and Lady Crawford has the rare quality (especially rare in women, I would venture to say) of being able to think big. She doesn't peck at her gardening, popping a plant in wherever she can see a gap. Her groupings are always large and generous, so that they can create the landscape effects, with broad brush-strokes, that are needed. And no one could be better aware of the importance of good foliage, whether it be light and feathery, as with ferns and astilbes, or massive, as with rheums, bergenias and acanthus. On the other hand, she loves the sort of plants that show their appreciation of the conditions they find themselves in by self-sowing. This, largely, is what integrates a garden and gives to it a lived-in, loved appearance and atmosphere; the personal stamp of belonging.

I shall try to describe Lady Crawford's style of gardening with examples. But first I should explain that she was Swiss born and bred and did no gardening while she lived in Switzerland. This started when she owned her first garden, in Hampstead. She and her husband also built themselves a holiday home near to Balcarres and she made a large garden there, already planting generously and for effect. Then came Balcarres, where she has worked – and

Ruth's Garden. The yellow and white sections, liberally strengthened with good foliage.

A buttress, turned pot, with a prosperous house leek (*Sempervivum*).

she is nothing if not a hands-on gardener – for some fifteen years. Donald Lamb has been her head gardener for all that time and there is one assistant. An extra pair of hands is really needed.

Near to the house is a prettily designed, formally laid out rose garden, with a central fountain and octagonal pool (dry, for as long as I have known them!), the surrounding beds edged with stone seats. Roses are there, but diluted by so much other planting that you are not aware of the ugly habit of the Hybrid Tea. In spring there are tulips. Pansies and golden feverfew sow themselves, freely. Catmint, always a winner when combined with the first flowering of bush roses in June, is the 'Six Hills' strain, and I have never seen it looking so bright. Cushion plants like pinks and lamb's lugs (*Stachys lanata*) lap over the stone margins. Cranesbills feature strongly throughout the garden (I was impressed in a wild bit by pink *Geranium endressii* in front of a yellow tree lupin) and are here represented by the months-long-flowering 'Russell Prichard', which is unashamed magenta, and 'Buxton's Variety' of the blue and white *G. wallichianum*. Blue flax does well and there is a range of penstemons. Agapanthus contribute to the late summer scene, while in winter, small evergreens like hebes, lavender cotton and rue keep the interest alive.

Rosa rugosa 'Fru Dagmar Hastrup' with blue aquilegias.

The beds are heavily mulched with cow manure from the farm. Throughout the garden there is evidence, from plant growth, of generous feeding.

The Rose Garden is in an area enclosed on three sides by walls, that furthest from the main building being known as the Dower House. There is some pretty planting alongside and in front of this (though Lady Crawford is never quite satisfied and is always on the lookout for ideas for further improvements). For instance, the pink Rugosa rose 'Fru Dagmar Hastrup' has pink and blue long-spurred columbines flowering in front of and through it. These were originally a mixture, but Lady Crawford eliminated the yellow and red shades. Columbines make large and thoroughly perennial plants in the north, and grow 3–4 feet tall.

There is a charming corner where a paved path rises a few steps, leads on to a bay window in the Dower House, then turns aside to a conservatory. This does give a cottagey feeling and is treated in that way. The bright pink *Geranium palmatum*, which is generally monocarpic, maintains itself abundantly, here, by self-seeding. A climbing David Austin rose, 'The Alchemist', with flat-faced, apricot blooms packed with petals, grows to one side of the window and a very healthy *Clematis* 'Duchess of Edinburgh' on the other, that being double white. At the entrance to this little garden, a lowish wall ends in a kind of buttress-cum-pot, on the ledge of whose pedestal grows a prosperous house leek (sempervivum). It was flowering in September. There's a huge swathe of *Geranium wallichianum* 'Buxton's Variety' to one side.

Near by is the vegetable and fruit garden, and a large, square area, which used to be a lawn. All of this Lady Crawford engaged James Russell to design for her, when she first came to live at Balcarres. It is a happy sequel that Mr Russell, who then lived at Castle Howard in Yorkshire and did much brilliant work for the late Lord Howard, is now a near neighbour, having built a house on Balcarres land. He can be consulted at any time.

The planting of this new area, known as Ruth's Garden, is all Lady Crawford's. You approach it from one corner, where the view is blocked by a large shrub (there is one on each corner), so it is a pleasure to discover what lies behind – a parterre with a willow-leaved weeping pear in the centre and four box-edged beds around it, each having its own colour theme. There is no rigidity about this and certain plants are repeated in two or three beds, the contents of which include shrubs as well as perennials. 'It's difficult to find enough apricot flowers,' Lady Crawford observed of the plot devoted mainly to this colour. Aquilegias and oriental poppies are principal ingredients in June, together with roses 'Apricot Nectar' and 'Perle d'Or', foxgloves and apricot-coloured shrubby potentillas.

Some flowers, notably aquilegias and violas, self-sow into beds where their colour is 'wrong'. 'I can't bring myself to pull them out, but I *will*,' Lady Crawford declared. She won't! I love to see the way that *Viola cornuta* (especially, but other violas and pansies behave the same way) climbs into its neighbours. The pure white form, 'Alba', keeps pace for quite a time with the young growth of a late-flowering herbaceous phlox (*Phlox paniculata*). A number of the shrubs are shaped into balls or cones, which adds to the interest, though the accents intended from 'Skyrocket' junipers are a sad let-down, as this wretched variety loses its natural shape after a very few years and has to be bound together to stop it falling apart. I think the spire-like, small-leaved holly, *Ilex aquifolium* 'Hascombensis', would be a good choice for this purpose, but it is rather slow-growing. That is tiresome in the early years, but makes for a solid shrub in the long run.

I have one criticism of Ruth's Garden. I think it tries to cover too long a season of interest and this is at the expense of any potential climax. From midsummer on, there are a lot of passengers. Lupins, in selected shades, feature in all four beds and they look fine in June, but what's to be done about them when the phloxes and tiger lilies are out? Of early flowerers like epimediums and pulmonarias, you can say that their foliage is an asset all through the summer, but it is of a kind that would better suit a woodland walk, where, indeed, they feature strongly at Balcarres. But that's just my opinion.

Lady Crawford's woodland and semi-woodland plantings are the most successful of all. She keeps on extending her dominion in the direction of treed areas. First, and adjacent to Ruth's Garden, is the Tennis Woodland. Its cedars form a background to Ruth's Garden and it slopes fairly steeply down

Tree lupins and *Geranium endressii* in a semi-wild area.

to a discreetly located tennis court. There is a good bit of light beneath and at the edge of the tree canopy (sycamore and horse chestnut as well as cedar) and the plantings are rich. Shrubs are fairly low-growing and don't block the view, such as *Daphne mezereum*, shrubby euphorbias, tree lupins, a score of shrub roses and *Helleborus argutifolius*, which makes quite tall colonies, enviably healthy (mine are pathetic) and showing no inclination to fall apart.

'The Tennis Woodland,' Lady Crawford wrote me after seeing my first draft of this piece, 'is dedicated to my grandchildren; it's *their* garden. I feel what you *own* you care for. I want them to learn to *love* it, to *love* plants, *love* to want to garden one day, not now. To make it easy for them, I planted almost only scented plants, especially bordering the paths, and I encourage them to squeeze them to release the scent. We have picnics there whenever they are here; we sit on the herbs surrounding the sitting area in the middle of the Tennis Garden and we cook soup there and risotto, on the open wood fire and then we watch them play tennis – all in *their* garden. I think and hope it works.' The herbs she mentions are golden balm, golden marjoram and thyme. Masses of the autumn flowering *Cyclamen hederifolium* run right through this woodland, happily naturalizing.

The plants are given a good start, kept weeded and otherwise allowed to get on with it, many of them self-sowing: Jacob's ladder (*Polemonium caeruleum*), foxgloves, columbines, wild moon daisies, red and white valerian in the sunnier spots, hardy cyclamen. These are a few examples. *Campanula lactiflora*, one of the tallest of its genus, is an excellent colonizer and flowers in July, whereas the intense blue *Omphalodes cappadocica* makes a large colony and has a long spring-flowering period. *Lamium maculatum* 'White Nancy' is one of the most satisfactory for lighting up shady places with its white flowers and so is *L. m.* 'Aureum' for its leaves, though I noticed this particularly in another part of the garden. In the south, its foliage is inclined to scorch, but not here. The scented perennial honesty, *Lunaria rediviva*, is here and several herbaceous spurges, including *Euphorbia coralloides*, which makes bold lime green inflorescences only 15 inches to 2 feet tall and self-sows generously. Geraniums, of course; as I remarked before, they are everywhere. Here I noticed *G. endressii*, which I like quite as much as any of the hybrids derived from it; pink *Geranium macrorrhizum*, which is evergreen and admirable ground cover in difficult, dark places; *G. phaeum*, weedy-looking, with small, near black flowers – one of my least favourites.

If you go through the vegetable garden, out of a gate and across a ride, you find yourself in one of Lady Crawford's later extensions (but not the last of them, believe me). This is a very open woodland garden, known as Mary's Walk, notable for large and sumptuous plantings. Never, for instance, have I

Foxgloves give structure to a planting otherwise dominated by mounded cranesbills.

seen the glossy foliage of *Bergenia* 'Ballawley' looking more prosperous, and this was backed, in June, by the seething mass of tiny pink flowers of *Rosa farreri persetosa* (now *R. elegantula*), coming right down to the bergenia's level. Improbable but charming. Things like cimicifugas and *Kirengeshoma palmata* are a foliar feast long before they flower. They thrive so much better here than with me, partly because of climate, which I can't help, but more than I care to admit because they are so well looked after and fed. The kirengeshoma was already $3\frac{1}{2}$ feet tall in June. Filipendulas, the meadowsweet tribe, love it. I do enjoy the virulent magenta of *Filipendula purpurea*. It has such vitality. It is a modest 4 feet tall but a white one – could it be *F. kamtschatica*? – was a good 8 feet. It was found growing 'wild' in nearby woods.

There are doronicums and pulmonarias to flower in spring and a double pink cherry makes an umbrella above blue *Omphalodes verna*. My burnt orange *Euphorbia griffithii* 'Dixter' looked good, I thought, near to a sunny swathe of *Philadelphus coronarius* 'Aureus'. For best foliage effect, this benefits from a hard annual cut-back, in winter. You thereby sacrifice the flowers, but there are plenty of other mock oranges for them. From a plant originally given her by her dressmaker, Lady Crawford worked up stock of the bladder fern, *Cystopteris fragilis*, till she could plant it in a big group, each unit of which was making its individual mark. The deciduous fronds have great delicacy.

So there are many contrasts of texture and form. In the background, a group of three *Viburnum rhytidophyllum*, the wrinkled texture of whose large, evergreen leaves can make of it such a handsome feature when it is growing lustily, as here (it can look miserable, when unhappy). Clearly her plants were all of the same clone, as they haven't borne crops of the handsome berries, red at first, then red and black, finally black, of which it is capable if genetically different plants are grown near to each other. The answer, in this case, is to buy or raise seedlings.

Walk on a bit further and you come to some of the latest plantings, along both sides of the main approach drive, where only nettles grew before. *Rodgersia podophylla* was rampant, here, its foliage already taking on autumn tints in mid-September. I was also pleased to see one of my favourite astilbes, the elegant white 'Professor van de Wielen'. The trunks of yew trees have been cleaned up, allowing underplantings of such deep shade tolerators as *Geranium macrorrhizum* 'Album' and the hard shield fern, *Polystichum aculeatum*. This native was growing wild on a steep bank elsewhere on the property (it seems to favour steep banks), so Lady Crawford transferred some of it. *Cyclamen hederifolium* have come from other parts of the garden. Where she wants to establish them around the trunk of a tree, for instance, and there is competition from grass, she can apply a herbicide in summer, when the cyclamen are dormant.

Across the drive, a bowl-shaped expanse of woodland has been cleared and has become her sunshine area. Having a dark background, plants like golden privet and the giant yellow daisy *Inula magnifica* show up dramatically from a distance. But things will change, as newly planted pines grow up. On this side of the road there are some splendid old shrubs. Most of the old, grafted rhododendrons have reverted to their *ponticum* stock, but this makes a lovely display in June. There is a *Cornus kousa* in its prime. You have to get into just the right position to admire its white blossom, in June, because there is a lot of undergrowth. An immense *Stranvaesia davidiana* (now removed by the botanists to *Photinia*) billows in folds, and there are trees of eucryphia.

There was another edge-of-woodland planting that I admired, taking a different route back towards the house, this in early autumn, with the dark, purplish backcloth of the elder, *Sambucus nigra* 'Guincho Purple', highlighting a yellow-berried pyracantha, the red clustered fruit of guelder rose, *Viburnum opulus*, and the luminous foliage of golden privet – such a good shrub when allowed to grow freely. Which doesn't mean you should never take the saw or secateurs to it but that it looks better when not a tight ball or regularly clipped hedge.

These woodland areas have many new rhododendron plantings and their appearance will change radically as the rhododendrons mature. Whether entirely for the good remains to be seen. The results may be more stolid.

If you look out from the house towards the Bass Rock, there are areas of lawn beyond the Rose Garden and then a balustrade. A weeping Camperdown wych elm, *Ulmus glabra* 'Camperdownii', which had for many years been a key feature on one of the plats, was rapidly dying of the dread disease when I last saw it. The question was, with what does one replace it? This aroused a lot of discussion and the answer is not easy to find, as the position is exposed. I don't know what decision has been come to, but at the time we (it was, of course, Lady Crawford's idea) agreed that a *Cercidiphyllum japonicum* might be a good solution. This tree grows particularly well in Scotland and there is a wonderful, many-stemmed, bowl-shaped specimen in the woodland here. It makes a beautifully shaped tree, has charming orbicular foliage and often changes to pinkish tones before shedding its leaves in autumn. The fallen foliage smells of caramel.

Below the balustrade is a very big drop to the Lower Garden (but there are balustraded steps down, the severity of these softened by self-sowing red valerian). The walls creating and supporting this structure are something like 20 feet at their highest. As the aspect is sunny, there is inviting scope for wall plantings.

The fruitily scented *Cytisus battendieri* is usually treated as a wall specimen (there is no good reason why), but quickly reaches beyond the top and has to be cut back, and that removes potential flowering wood. Here, it has the necessary head height. So does *Abutilon vitifolium*, a soft shrub of immense vigour. Not long-lived but quickly replaced, and you can have it in mauve or white. A *Cotoneaster horizontalis* belies its name and grows 20 feet up the wall and so does *Garrya elliptica*, cherished for its midwinter grey-green catkins. A purple-leaved *Prunus cerasifera* 'Pissardii' is trained into the wall, instead of being allowed to grow as a tree. That flowers all right, I am told, and it has a summer-flowering clematis growing over it. A black mulberry is also trained as a wall specimen, but does nothing.

Where the wall is only 9 feet high, there is a 15-foot deep mixed border in front of it, but where it is 20 feet, buttresses of yew hedging have been grown at regular intervals along the front of it. Each compartment so formed contains a specimen shrub rose in the centre, underplanted with a harmonizing ground cover plant. Thus the pink Hybrid Musk 'Cornelia' is surrounded by 'Johnson's Blue' cranesbills and the pink *Escallonia* 'Langelyensis' is more or less against the wall behind. Sometimes, as in this case, the idea works well, sometimes less so. I fancy the yew roots have an inhibiting effect on plantings that are so close to them.

The one skeleton in the garden's cupboard is a parterre in the lower garden, edged in mangy box and steeped, no doubt, in tradition. It needs taking by the scruff and throwing out. Something will happen one day. Meantime, as town planners also find, it's more rewarding to start from scratch than to have to tinker with or around old features.

For there is another, recent, extension, five minutes' walk from the house, where a lovely pond, in a hollow, is being made even more beautiful. All this is Lady Crawford's and Donald Lamb's work. Everyone else said STOP, and that it was too much, and it was a struggle, but their enthusiasm and determination have carried all before them – on a shoestring. All the shrubs and perennials have been home-propagated. There was a big drift, in September, of *Polygonum campanulatum*, which I specially admired; it was not merely prolific in bloom but an unusually rich shade of pink. Climate? Strain? I don't know.

Now Lady Crawford's eldest son and daughter-in-law have built a house in the Umbrian hills, with 6 acres of land around. The surroundings are wonderful, and the wild flowers, but she and Donald Lamb have taken loads of plants, specially propagated and made ready, out from Balcarres. 'There is no end to the fun we have handling plants and creating beauty with and through them,' my friend writes. 'You will understand – it's intoxicating, isn't it?'

That's how gardening should be.

FRENICH

———◆———

FRENICH is bang in the middle of Scotland. I have been visiting there almost annually for many years. That, in a way, makes it more difficult to write about, as all my notes and photographs are scattered and by the time I've got a grip on one thing, it turns out to have slipped out of my grasp and to have turned into something else. Which is the sign of a garden that doesn't stand still but is always developing. Its owner is a plantsman but he is always looking at and reassessing the more generalized scene. In the courtyard that is surrounded by three sides of his house, rectangular areas within the paving were planted up with *Rosa sericea omeiensis* 'Pteracantha', the one whose large thorns are so luminous, on the young shoots, when transfused by low sunlight. I have a vivid recollection of giving those roses a mighty pruning, and there was a singularly successful pink 'Hagley Hybrid' clematis draped over one bush. It's years, now, since that lot was all replaced but I remember them more clearly than the replacements, which are bamboos, I *think*. They are more suitable, having more personality, given the architectural setting. Colin used to grow a lot of roses; now very few. He can see, as so many, blinded by sentiment, cannot, that taking them year round, most are an insulting wreckage for most of the time.

However, to go back to the beginning. Colin Hamilton and Kulgin Duval are dealers in antiquarian books and they work from home. Colin is the gardener. They bought Frenich in 1969, but serious gardening did not start for several years after that.

Nine miles from Pitlochry, in Perthshire, Frenich is on a narrow, wooded lane running alongside Loch Tummel. Car-parking would be so impossible that opening the garden to the public would simply not be on (supposing they wanted to). The land rises steeply, behind, and all is on a north slope, the sun disappearing for months in winter. Nevertheless, thanks to the loch, the feeling is of openness.

The climate, in winter, is pretty unpleasant – Colin calls it impossible –

and can be severe, by British standards. One winter, Colin was able to walk right across the loch, over snow and ice. That must be a mile, or so. One year, the ground didn't thaw out till April. Since then, they've built a house in Kerala, south India, and escape there from November to April, leaving Douglas, a dog and two cats to look after Frenich in their absence. I only ever visit in June or September, so have never seen the birches glowing in late autumn, but from the garden's point of view, I have a pretty good idea of what goes on.

The present house was a tumbledown farmsteading when Colin and Kulgin purchased it. There was a byre for cows, stalls for four horses, a mill-wheel for the threshing machine and a granary. Above what is now the garage, there was a bothy. Otherwise this is a single-storey stone building (everything is of stone in these parts), E-shaped without the centre of the E. The ground below the long side of the E slopes down to a burn, the noise of which makes a satisfactory background, loud or soft, to living. So different from the contrived tinkle that many lowland gardeners fancy, from company's water recirculated by a pump.

Some of the best of the garden lies on the other side of this burn, and the land had to be purchased from their neighbour. To reach it, they built a hump-backed wooden bridge. Any such construction has to take note of the ferocious strength of water when the burn is in spate. The bridge leads to a summerhouse. Only 20 or so yards upstream is the delightful old stone road bridge, through which you can see to burn and woodland beyond.

The burn, flanked by ash trees and alders, flattens out alongside a meadow and quickly reaches its brief, gravelly estuary, where it debouches into the loch. These are enviable features to have in your middling-sized garden, though always with the problems of flood water and its tendency to sweep away any features that are within its reach.

Colin Hamilton is someone who works quickly and efficiently (he is an excellent cook) without appearing to do so. He is great for getting things done, but without fuss. His time is constantly interrupted (for instance, by visits from people like me); even in summer, he seems to be away as much as he is at home, but the garden is always under control. Of course, he does have Douglas there (he didn't always) and he is a great support. Kulgin doesn't pretend to be a gardener (one is quite enough in most homes), but sometimes weeds.

Colin's wits are sharp, he asks the right questions and he is never without a notebook, whether in his own garden or in another or visiting a nursery. He gets carried away and buys a great many plants. However, before buying, he does make sensible inquiries about a plant's requirements, so as to decide

The garden from the road. Loch Tummel behind.

whether it's likely to be right for him, and of those he acquires, quite a remarkable number settle down and thrive. They are often plants that most of us find difficult. One of the most surprising things about his garden is that its frequent ecological rule-breaking, far from being punished, actually works. Shade-lovers and sun-lovers get on a treat, grown side by side, the moisture-lovers with those preferring dry conditions. This astonishes Beth Chatto, on her visits. She has strong precepts on what is ecologically correct and is a little disturbed when the lion lies down with the lamb.

What it really boils down to is that you adapt your gardening to the conditions you find (though to an extent these can be modified), and you learn as you go along. Here, the soil is acid, stony and well-drained. If fed, it grows plants well, but even summer temperatures are fairly low (which suits some plants) and the growing season is short. The sun seldom blazes unkindly and plants with yellow leaves don't often scorch. Drought will always be a problem, on occasion. However high your annual rainfall, plants will develop expectations that are sometimes betrayed. Colin irrigates. He is a pragmatist and he takes trouble.

On the house walls, there used to be a Victoria plum (much the most successful variety in Scotland) and morello cherry. Both were successful, at times, but have long since gone, as have the vegetables in the enclosed walled garden. There are more important things, which don't happen to be edible. One of the best-colouring *Actinidia kolomikta*, in pink, white and green, that I have seen grows against the east wall of the house, and there is a vigorous 'Bill Mackenzie' clematis, hung with its yellow lantern flowers for a long season. Bushing forwards but benefiting from the wall's proximity is a magnificent specimen – as good as I have seen – of *Piptanthus nepalensis*. It shows no sign of the dieback that is so frequent in the south. This is a fairly large, bulging, semi-evergreen shrub with trifoliate leaves and a blue-green sheen on the young stems that remind me of some bamboo canes. The clusters of yellow pea flowers are quite substantial and open over a longish period in early summer.

On the south wall there used to be a wisteria, but these are frequently none too free-flowering in Scotland and it didn't grow very heartily, either. So that was replaced by a male and a female *Schisandra rubriflora*, first admired in my garden. The lady fruits much more freely for Colin than ever she did for me, even before mine pined and almost died. The flowers, in May, are waxy red lampshades while the red berries, in September, are displayed vertically along an elongated axis. Theirs is a prolonged display and have won this species its Award of Merit from the RHS, whereas the flowers, which are diluted by rather a lot of foliage, have not.

Looking across the burn to the house.

The east side of the house is important, as this is the principal sitting- and eating-out area, close to the kitchen and to a door from the dining-room itself. There are large, informal beds around here. The heights to which plants grow is rather amazing and often means (as with delphiniums, *Thalictrum delavayi* and *Campanula lactiflora*, which runs up to 8 feet with ease) that efficient support is needed.

Bowles's golden sedge, *Carex elata* 'Aurea', takes on its brightest yellow colouring in a sunny position and contrasts well with a purple viola near to it. These violas have a climbing habit, when given the chance. One such had hoisted itself quite a way up the deciduous *Escallonia virgata*. Mauve and white forms of *Viola cornuta* are prolific down the slope, mixing well with the 2-foot spires of a good strain of *Verbascum phoeniceum*, in shades of white, pinky grey, lilac pink and purple. However, these are not as perennial as the violas and don't self-sow much, so they are dying out. Blue Jacob's ladder, *Polemonium caeruleum*, is certainly not, self-sowing freely. Its blue flower heads grow quite 4 feet tall, here, and also look good with lilies.

Poppies are a great success. Colin has lots of the *Papaver orientale* cultivars. He allowed me to take root cuttings from one with salmon flowers that I admired in June, when it was in bloom, and they have done splendidly for me, although summer isn't the usual time for propagating in this way. *P. rupifragum*, with its low rosettes of grey-green foliage and apricot flowers on quite long scapes, can be a bit of a weed but seems not to be a nuisance at Frenich, where it is represented by the semi-double form, 'Flore Pleno'. Yellow Welsh poppies seed everywhere.

Predictably, many meconopsis are in their element, as in so many Scottish gardens, the cool climate and damp atmosphere suiting them to perfection. Colin has a prosperous colony of a pretty blue strain of *M.* × *sheldonii*, probably 'Branklyn', and that finds itself in surprising juxtaposition with a pink oriental, which one somehow thinks of in a different, non-woodlandy style of planting. There is a great fat clump of the graceful *M. quintuplinervis*, whose lilac flowers arch over on slender stalks. The recently reintroduced, pure-red-flowered but quite low-growing species, *M. punicea*, also seems to be holding its own and in one case to be perennial. The main stock has been raised from seed from his own plants.

Most of the meconopsis (and Colin has a number of the monocarpic types with handsome rosettes of hairy foliage in the pre-flowering years) are at their best before my arrival in June, but *M. chelidonifolia* comes later and I like its scalloped leaves and graceful habit, quite apart from the smallish lemon yellow flowers, which are charming. He also grows a number of other poppy relatives like *Stylophorum diphyllum*, whose yellow flowers are supported by pinnate leaves with oak-leaf-like pinnae.

Much of the lushest, semi-woodland planting is on the terraced bank just the other side of the burn. I would have expected the climate to be too harsh for *Gunnera manicata*, but you couldn't wish for a healthier-looking specimen,

Left, *Meconopsis grandis* and pink oriental poppies with the burn behind.

Right, globe flowers (*Trollius yunnanensis*) taking advantage of the light before the burnside *Gunnera manicata* takes over completely.

down by the burnside and just the far side of the bridge. It has golden yellow globe flowers (*Trollius*), flowering spryly beneath the expanding gunnera foliage in late spring. A May-flowering combination that must look good is of the mauve, parsley-like *Chaerophyllum hirsutum* 'Roseum' with the 3-foot globe heads of *Allium aflatunense*, also mauve but of totally different form.

Lilies are happy and I saw little sign of damage by botrytis. I counted 133 blooms/buds on a single spray of a pink *Lilium speciosum* hybrid (quite small-flowered), one September. *L. duchartrei* has shown its pleasure by making a wide-spreading stoloniferous group. *L. mackliniae*, grown by Colin from seed, has developed some strong-flowering bulbs. It comes close, in relationship, to *Nomocharis*. *N. mairei* is the species with which he is having greatest success. White and purple *L. martagon* self-sow. Hardy orchids are excellent, notably *Dactylorhiza × grandis*, whose solid spikes are a good, rich mauve, and the reddish purple *D. maderense*. The slipper orchid, *Cypripedium reginae*, looks happy enough, though not yet approaching the clump in Helen Dillon's garden (see page 158).

There are generous colonies of many perennials, most of them moisture-loving. Rodgersias, for instance, three kinds of *Actaea*, two with white berries, one with red. The tall, glaucous-leaved *Thalictrum flavum glaucum* seems very much at home but so does the far more difficult *T. chelidonii*, $3\frac{1}{2}$ feet tall, with large mauve flowers and delicate foliage. Such a refined plant; it doesn't relish the comparatively hot south of England at all. *Iris sibirica* and *I. chrysographes*, in its night purple form, grow abundantly. An excellent autumn combination is made with the blue willow gentian. *Gentiana asclepiadea*, and the lemon yellow shuttlecocks and maple leaves (their black stems also good) of *Kirensgeshoma palmata*. An organic piece of bronze sculpture by Edward Mansfield springs from a rock and gives body to this scene.

Colin doesn't yield to the temptation of overdoing hostas, which are ideally suited, not losing their lustre in late summer, as they so often do after a hot spell in the south. 'Gold Edger' and the glaucous 'Halcyon' still look very fresh in September. Ferns grow splendidly and they are appreciated as they deserve. The maidenhair, *Adiantum pedatum*, seems as though it ought to be a native.

There are shrubs, of course, but Colin takes care that they shan't steal the perennials' thunder. If, like *Paeonia lutea ludlowii*, they grow oversize without justifying the space, out they go. He has *Salix helvetica* and *S. lanata*, both neat, grey-leaved shrubs, but the former has the greater style. *S. exigua*, so silvery and slender to 10 feet or more, is a great pleasure. These willows do not need so much sunshine as the majority of greys to give of their best, and they are born to a moist, cool climate, which the majority of greys are anything but.

I was pleased to see *Sambucus canadensis* 'Maxima' making such a fine display in September. It is great for lengthening the season. So do white Japanese anemones and late red crocosmias. Geraniums seem to be everywhere, in June, especially the forms of *Geranium pratense*, which seed with embarrassing freedom.

Peonies and foxgloves in the rectangular walled enclosure.

A plant that I should not have expected to do so well, in the circumstances, is *Crambe cordifolia*, but it is very free. Not so tall as usual, which is an advantage; 5 feet is quite enough. It doesn't come into flower until the end of June. Tall yellow verbascums grow near to it, and white foxgloves. They are abundant in many places and Colin is ruthless in rooting out all the magenta ones the moment they show up. Not many do, these days.

I shall return to the burnside in a moment. Meantime the curious, fairly high, rectangular walled stone enclosure that used to be a vegetable garden is now packed with ornamentals. *Buddleia* 'Dartmoor' grows cheek by jowl with a tremendously vigorous *Berberis temolaica*, which I should somehow never have expected to do so well in this climate, seeing that its leaves are glaucous and, one would have thought, suited to moisture-evaporating conditions. The buddleia flowers in September and receives little direct sunshine by then. I never saw a butterfly near it. *Paeonia lactiflora* hybrids made a great show in June and contrast well with more white foxgloves.

A gate at the far end of this garden takes you on to the burnside at a lower level than where we were examining the plants just now. Here Colin keeps things simple, the margins being covered with grey river-bed gravel, few plants intervening, though there are more foxgloves and martagon lilies; on a raised bed, white honesty among deciduous azaleas. I have not seen them blooming but doubt whether they would be in the raucous colour combinations that one so often quails before.

A path running parallel with the burn (still alders and ashes alongside it) leads you down to the loch. The blue perennial cornflower, *Centaurea montana*, *Polemonium caeruleum*, pink *Geranium endressii*, *Alchemilla mollis* and martagon lilies, both white and purple, have all established well in meadow grass here.

Then you are in a boggy area, the estuary, right out in the open (and very exposed it is), bar a clump of native goat willow bushes. Colin has been struggling to establish a bog garden here for some years now, and he is winning through, the chief obstacle being the maverick behaviour of the burn when there's a spate. We think that steps taken to control this are working, but you never quite know with such an irrepressible force.

Certain plants are doing very well and the exposed situation makes them grow sturdily. The flat-headed, deep mauve *Eupatorium maculatum* 'Atropurpureum' seems to have a good hold on the situation and was covered with dozy bumble-bees when I saw it in damp, chilly weather. As I noted at Balcarres, *Persicaria campanulata* seems to have a much richer pink colouring than I am used to. Whether this is a deep form or whether the exposed conditions make it so, I am not sure, but it certainly suits the plant. I should like to see this area a thoroughgoing success, as I believe it was I who originally encouraged Colin to attempt it.

Few Scottish gardens are without alpines; the climate and the rocks suit them. Colin accommodates them on the south side of the house. First there is a flat, raised bed for them, running alongside the path that flanks the house (this was a fairly recent switch from deciduous azaleas). Then, on a steeply rising bank behind, a scree has been made. So there is plenty of scope for these plants. Most Scottish nurserymen concentrate on alpines.

Whether you like a garden best for its plants or for the way in which they have been displayed, Frenich is stimulating and a great deal can be learned from what Colin has achieved. He hasn't stopped yet.

HOUSE OF GRUINARD

———◦———

O NE OF MY TWO most battered 1-inch maps, dating from 1963, when first I visited the area, takes in the north-west Scottish coastline from Gairloch, northwards to the Summer Isles at the mouth of Loch Broom. I have returned every year but one, since then. It is wonderful walking country; the map would be stuffed into my anorak pocket, a compass in the haversack over my shoulder. Sometimes the weather is spooky and inhospitable but overall I connect my days of hiking in those wild parts, where to see anyone was unusual, with a sense of freedom and elation.

Gruinard House is in the centre of this coastline, sitting just below the A432, a single track road when I first knew it. The house is on the east side of Gruinard Bay (Gruinard, incidentally, is pronounced something like Grinyard), and although this faces north, the garden itself looks only a few points west of south. It is sandwiched in a steeply falling $1\frac{1}{2}$-acre strip between the road and the estuary of the Gruinard River. Geologically, it is a raised beach, of which there are many on the west coast of Scotland, of highly porous sand, even to a depth of 2 feet. That is probably just as well, in view of high rainfall and the way water normally hangs around. The tall, white harled house is a little separated from the garden, whose main purpose was to provide vegetables for the house when the fishing and stalking seasons were on. Some big hulks of old, unpruned shrubs such as forsythia and escallonia, a pink astilbe and some 'Dorothy Perkins' rambler roses were just about its only contents.

The Hon. Mrs Angus (Jane) Maclay is the present owner and the property was her mother's, father's and grandfather's before her, but it is the energy and plantsmanship of their gardener, Fiona Clark, which has transformed the place over the past twenty-five years or so.

To be so near to the river estuary, literally only a stone's throw away, is quite exciting. At high tide, salt water is gently lapping the garden's boundary, yet the estuary is so short and the terrain so steep that the noise of the river's

June luxuriance, with many hardy perennials. Orange *Primula bulleyana* is fronted by blue cranesbills.

last waterfalls sounds loud in your ears. In quiet weather, it doesn't even feel exposed. There are plenty of trees around, especially beeches along the roadside boundary. But gales are of the fiercest, in these parts, and shelter is the gardener's first concern. There were willows and sea buckthorn, to which Fiona added flowering currant, but the chief barrier immediately along the garden's lower margin is a dense hedge of the evergreen daisy bush, *Olearia × haastii*. This is, in my opinion, one of the dullest members of its genus, but it does an excellent job and, at its flowering in late summer, is quite a sight – a mass of small white blossom. Having flowered, it is immediately cut back to ensure that it remains a hedge. This means that it spends the next year making young growth on which to flower the year after. So flowering is biennial.

Another shrub from the same part of Australasia that is much used here for its comely silver-grey evergreen foliage and dense growth when kept trim is *Brachyglottis* 'Sunshine', more familiarly *Senecio laxifolius* or *S. greyi*. Again, Fiona cuts it back in early autumn and it refurnishes the following spring. Where winters are harder, this wouldn't do; you'd wait till spring to prune, but here, the maritime climate and mild, prevailing south-westerlies make the difference. Where, in background areas, Fiona can afford to allow enjoyment of the jolly, early summer display of bright yellow daisies, she leaves growth untrimmed for a second season.

She is keen on hardy perennials, of which there were virtually none on her arrival, and even raises surplus stock for a nearby nursery, also selling plants from Gruinard on their three annual openings, each May, June and July, in aid of the Scottish National Gardens Scheme. This is an excellent garden in early autumn, too. Not only is there plenty of family around, then, but Fiona enjoys the season. 'I love autumn,' she told me when I was there in late September. 'It's very colourful anyway; you just add a few bits and pieces. It's not so frantic as in spring,' Hear, hear. But late autumn flowers, like some of the bugbanes (*Cimicifuga*) get copped by gales and frequently fail to make it. Kaffir lilies, *Schizostylis coccinea*, succeed, if frequently divided (I find they need that, too) and look well among the crocus yellow sprays of *Crocosmia* 'Citronella', another genus that needs frequent division to keep it from going blind.

Two parallel paths run the garden's length, the lower alongside the olearia hedge, the upper beneath the roadside trees. Connecting paths, running up and down the slope, subdivide the central area. One of these alleys is a pergola, made of larch posts, on which grow honeysuckle and rambler roses, including the old-fashioned 'Goldfinch'. Beneath, and for autumn flowering, is a double row of the hardy red-and-purple fuchsia 'Mrs Popple'. This is treated as herbaceous, being cut to the ground each winter. Another alley is lined with deciduous azaleas, whose autumn colour makes almost as bright an impact as the flowers in May. The last alley, at the garden's far end, is little used and Fiona encourages its natural mantle of mosses.

The large plot near to the start of the garden grows vegetables, flowers for picking and a massive colony of rhubarb. It is hard to imagine a Scottish garden, derelict or otherwise, without this great survivor. Potatoes flourish and do not suffer from root eelworm (nematodes). Brassicas, on the other hand, are liable to club root. The house cooks have, in general, been none too adventurous, so a vegetable like kohlrabi is seldom favoured. Sweet peas (for cutting), 'Hurst's Greenshaft' and mangetout peas are beautifully grown and well supported with brushwood and sheep's netting. If not immediately required, much of this produce goes into the deep freeze. The mangetouts have to be picked young and almost daily, if they are not to go stringy. 'I keep up with them for three weeks and then they get away from me,' said Fiona. I'm not keen on vegetables that are always breathing down my neck and threatening my conscience. Courgettes that turn in a twinkling into marrows are another example.

Plenty of support is also needed for a picking row of *Lavatera trimestris*

Autumn scene with intermingling *Crocosmia* 'Citronella' and *Schizostylis coccinea* 'Major'. Both flower better if frequently replanted.

'Silver Cup', a soft pink, large-flowered annual mallow. Can you imagine that 6 feet tall? But it was, and had just reached its peak in September.

Excellent growth is attained here and elsewhere. Fiona manures with seaweed, which is put on fresh, in autumn (the pong is considerable on warmer days), and used throughout the garden. Tons of farmyard manure is used annually and mulches of pine-needles, introduced in winter, are also applied to keep down weeds. For the introduction of these bulky ingredients, as also of rocks wherewith to build terracing, there is a side entrance off the road allowing the passage of a tractor and trailer. The materials are dumped a little way in and can be barrowed from there. Fiona has done a lot of construction with rock, much of it from the river bed. She put her boyfriend to working so hard, building terraces behind the pond, 'that he never talked to me again'. Tests of this kind should come early in a relationship.

The small pond occupies a key position in the lower central part of the garden. Previously, this area and that above it had merely been marshy, so it was a great thrill when Fiona discovered that there was a definite spring. She channelled this. The channel is open, making for easy clearance of debris. If closed, blockages would have given constant trouble. The water enters the pond at two points.

Sensibly the pond surface is kept open and clear. Anything like a waterlily would quickly obliterate the water, quite apart from the fact that many nymphaeas fail to bloom freely as far north as this. There is quite sufficient softening of the pond's margins by overhanging plants. Many moisture-loving

Plants fringing the little spring-fed pond. An orange mimulus in front.

Rodgersia podophylla, Primula 'Inverewe' and *Libertia formosa* in a wettish area.

primulas, particularly of the Sikkimensis and Candelabra groups. Theirs is the strongest contribution to the gaiety of the June scene. The darkness of *Iris chrysographes* 'Black Knight' is in suitable contrast.

The garden, in fact, is full of moisture-lovers, no special efforts on their behalf being needed. Double kingcups (*Caltha palustris*) flourish under normal border conditions and Fiona sells the surplus. The little double white *Ranunculus aconitifolius* 'Flore Pleno' is there, and the neat, double yellow buttercup, *R. acris* 'Flore Pleno' – 'really, really pretty' – is a favourite, though that will take quite dry conditions. It occurred to Fiona, as we walked round, that it would make a good companion for a smallish, semi-double orange geum she grows. It is very free over a long season and attractively floppy without becoming messy, as geums often tend to.

Rodgersia podophylla is not a free-flowering species, but a mere two or three of its large white panicles make their point near to the pond, while its foliage is coloured for most of the growing season, though brightest in autumn. One thinks of the water saxifrage on the same wavelength, *Darmera peltata*. Though it does not flower here, it colours magnificently with fiery tints in autumn. This seems to be characteristic, in Scotland, whereas in the south it merely dries up to an unattractive brown. Still, the foliage is an asset all through the growing season.

Astilbes are a great feature, flowering from June to October, according to variety. The short-stemmed, bright mauve *Astilbe chinensis pumila*, with its pointed panicles, contrasted well, in September, with the flat domes and rusty red colouring of *Sedum* 'Autumn Joy'. *Scrophularia auriculata* (*aquatica*)

'Variegata' is a marvellous foliage plant in moist soil, with its broad, white margins, if you can keep its enemies at bay. Slugs are the greatest menace in this climate, ruining the smooth, rounded leaves of *Ligularia clivorum*. This was such a reproach to me in my garden that I took the easy way out and stopped growing it. Around a *Veratrum viride*, Fiona found (and took, I believe) forty slugs in one square foot. But she prefers veratrums to hostas, by and large; they do have greater style. Hostas there are, of course, and it was good to see such a healthy colony of *Hosta crispula*, with its broad white leaf margin. Much of this, in the south, has gone down to virus disease.

A purple loosestrife, *Lythrum salicaria* 'Lady Sackville', was 7 feet tall. To the Americans, this species is an unmentionable pest of marshy areas, where it has completely taken over, and it is banned from gardens or for sale – a case of shutting the stable door after the horse has bolted, I should have thought. In its native habitats it presents no problems, finding, there, its natural checks, whatever they may be. Astrantias thrive, and Fiona loves Japanese anemones for the autumn, the simple white being her favourite (as also mine), though she welcomes the pink kinds, also. *Polygonum campanulatum* (*Persicaria campanulata*) grows so strongly as to need support. I bet she has to divide and control that, pretty frequently.

So much for the obvious moisture-lovers, and it will already be seen that Fiona has introduced a wide range of perennials. Of those without special moisture requirements, agapanthus are very happy and yield surplus stock for sales. There are many geraniums – a favourite group. In fact I felt a little queasy on seeing a bouncing colony of *Geranium procurrens*, rampaging without let or hindrance. Its purple, black-eyed flowers are a great sight in autumn, but it spreads like a strawberry, rooting at every node, and as the roots are taps, they are not readily extracted. However, the site was marginal and nothing can be said against a plant in its right place. It is all too easy to be dismissive of a willing colonizer, when it may be just the right choice for the circumstances.

Behind the pond, a little path meanders upwards, emerging into a small, cobbled area. In June I like the foliage contrast, here, between the sword leaves of crocosmias, with the scallops of *Alchemilla mollis* and multiply divided fern fronds. There are heathers, hereabouts. 'Gradually some of them are coming out; I don't mind them if they're doing well,' said Fiona. Certainly there were varieties of *Erica vagans* looking very handsome in September.

Shrubs and perennials are often worked in together to make mixed plantings, the shrubs, with their substance, being of particular value in the steeply rising top border, just below the road. Daisy bushes all do well, including the glamorous *Olearia semidentata*, with silvery undersides to its lance leaves and bold, purple flowers with even darker purple discs. And I like *O. capillaris*

Contrasts in leaf forms give pleasure long before flowers (if any) appear. *Alchemilla mollis* with crocosmia spears.

(though a hard winter finished mine off), with its neat, spoon-shaped leaves. That, like the majority, has white flowers, but *O.* × *zennorensis*, flourishing here as a foliage plant, never flowers at all, either here or with me in Sussex; only in Cornwall, where it originated (I am, of course, open to contradiction). We grow it for its grey-green lance leaves, which are margined with mock prickles and put me in mind of a well-furnished crocodile jaw.

Hebes are excellent. The small scimitar leaves, greyish green again, of *Hebe recurva*, on a neatly rounded bush of moderate size, looked smart, here. With me, it went into a too prolonged eclipse after flowering. Perhaps Fiona doesn't let hers flower or perhaps it doesn't want to. An unusual combination that appealed to me in the autumn was of the rich mauve *Hydrangea villosa*, whose branches reached to the ground and were there infiltrated by white shasta daisies. Behind them, the strong sword leaves of a New Zealand flax. Could it have been *Phormium cookianum*? It didn't look as hefty as *P. tenax*. There were bright, pinky mauve colchicums flowering in the foreground.

Here, as in all the best gardens, it is the work of a dedicated individual, in this case backed up, not thwarted, by her employers, which gives the place a feeling of vitality and continuing progress. Anything could happen, the visitor feels, and the urge is there to visit again and yet again. Such is the powerful germ of creativity. Well has gardening been called the sweet disease.

45 SANDFORD ROAD, DUBLIN

THE SORT OF garden I like best is full of healthy plants, so that, hungry to take everything in, I wonder which way to look. Many will be strange to me or such as I do not grow myself. The garden's design counts, of course; a flattering presentation of its contents depends largely on that, as also does the way the plants are arranged in relation to one another, but such matters are probably not what I notice first, being a self-confessed plantsman, first and foremost.

The moment I arrived at 45 Sandford Road, Dublin, on an early June afternoon, I knew that I was in for excitements. I was expecting no less, having read about it and having met Helen Dillon, the owner, at Dixter, so I came prepared to make copious notes with a view to writing this chapter, although the actual writing of it is, as matters have turned out, two and a half years later.

Beth Chatto and I had been asked to take part in a one-day gardening seminar, in Dublin, so we thought it a good idea to see a bit of Ireland together (especially the extraordinary limestone flora of the Burren, on the west coast), while we were about it. The seminar was the day after our arrival. We visited the Dillons within a short time of arriving and spent our last night there, nine days later.

45 Sandford Road is a four-square stone building with its main area of garden lying behind, but with a considerable apron of front garden, also. This, like the rest of the garden, has an open feel to it. Shade is cast by the house itself, on whose north side it is, but the necessary shelter which most gardeners crave for comes from neighbouring streets and gardens. The trees are there as a backdrop and they muffle the sound of traffic, but, not being in the garden itself, they have none of the nuisance value that trees in town gardens are apt to contribute – dripping branches, falling leaves, hungry roots; with deep shade and parched soil in summer.

Many of the beds and borders are raised a little, which makes for good drainage and is also an effective device for showing your plants off – display,

The garden has the benefit, beyond its boundary, of its neighbour's trees, which form a backdrop.

in fact. This is above all relevant to the numerous alpines, as is surfacing with a fine, grey gravel.

There is a raised bed immediately on your left as you enter, and behind the gateway pillar, a proud clump of *Stipa gigantea*, a grass that no one could miss noticing. I enjoy it above all when it is illuminated with a roseate glow by the setting sun. There are some plants, like this one, that I mention again and again in the gardens that I've visited, because I know them and I like them. I fear that, at the expense of plants with which I'm unfamiliar and have not, perhaps, sufficiently got to grips with to want to dilate on them, this may cause a certain monotony. I hope not, but I do remember that Percy Thrower, who for many years presented gardens on television for the BBC, would always seize on the 'Iceberg' rose for enthusiastic mention, even though it was of minimal importance in the garden concerned. It made him feel comfortable and he knew that his audiences would be able to relate to it, also. And, if not, they would have no difficulty in buying it.

In front of the stipa is a grey hummock of the woolliest of all lavenders, *Lavandula lanata* – too tender for me, alas. There was an excellent kniphofia hereabouts, with glaucous foliage like that of *K. caulescens*, but already running

Border mix on a raised bed with dwarf, bushy *Verbascum* 'Frosted Gold'. An early-flowering form of *Kniphofia caulescens* behind.

up to flower, which is far earlier than I've met in any other strain of this species. Anyway, it looked great. In front of it was one of those low, woolly, drainage-hungry mulleins, name of 'Frosted Gold'. Beautiful if you can make them happy and never whisper the word clay in their hearing. Pink dictamnus was flowering here and a pink erigeron, *E. philadelphicus*, which I'm sure I should know, judging by the number of its entries in *The Plant Finder*, but I didn't and I'm now too old to mind admitting my ignorance. (On second thoughts, I believe it is one that I have frequently met since I was a child of nine, but had never pinned a name to.) In a corner, a wonderful libertia hybrid, with graceful sprays of white flowers and much darker leaves than *L. formosa*, though of similar stature. Beth was enchanted with it, too, and Helen insisted on taking a piece off her only clump, which virtually entailed lifting the whole lot. As she had never propagated it before, this all seemed rather risky, but Beth's piece survived and multiplied and I now have some of it. This might be a vigorous form of *L. ixioides*.

Another group I fancied had *Yucca gloriosa* 'Variegata' – stiff as they come – with the ultra-glaucous *Euphorbia nicaeensis*, then in flower. I really must do that plant better; it's good the year round.

I continued fossicking around in this front area long after the others had gone through to the garden proper, on the south side of the house. Eventually my host, Mr Val Dillon, hauled me through. Smell of curry on the air; nine for dinner, that evening, but no sign of hurry or anxiety. I'm given an Irish whiskey, for fortification. I may say I have yet to learn the simultaneous arts of taking photographs, taking notes and holding a glass.

The Statue Garden. Its paving replaced a dirty little pool. *Clematis montana* behind.

Steps lead down, from a garden door, into the south garden and on to a sitting-out area, from which everywhere else is at a slightly higher level. You look out on a broad, central strip of lawn, edged with stone slabs. The lawn itself is perfectly kept and this is Val's province, as is much of the weeding. Not a weed in sight. The stone slabs mark the edge of borders, behind which are narrow paths and more borders. But there are also small enclosed areas, each with its own character. One has a sundial in the centre, another a pool, yet another a *putto*, with ornamental cobbles in a circle around it (this was converted from a grotty little pool). There are sunny areas and others to suit the shade-lovers, such as an alley of roses and clematis, giving shade to violets, bluebells, hellebores and a double *Polygonatum* (Solomon's seal). Helen is as strong on this genus as I am feeble. A few old apple trees also provide shade. One of them is shaped like an umbrella.

Before leaving the house behind us, I would remark on a *Bomarea caldasii* against it, already coming into flower. Mine starts a couple of months later. This is herbaceous and might be described as a sort of climbing alstroemeria. It is not hardy, but a good deal hardier than is generally supposed. So is *Rehmannia elata*, normally considered a conservatory pot plant but actually well worth planting out from seed-raised material. Its bright, pinky mauve funnels open widely into lobes at the mouth and are borne in racemes. That, too, was against the house. I was intrigued to see a *Solanum jasminoides* 'Album', a true climber, which had suckered into the paving and there made a non-climbing clump. A delightful tangle.

Standing with your back to the house, a path leads half right to a greenhouse

with benches and small things, like cushion androsaces that repay close exam-
ination. In fact there is a magnifying glass to facilitate this. Terrific splashes of
colour on the platform outside the greenhouse. For instance, a huge fleshy
mat-forming mesembryanthemum (technically *Delosperma*) covered with lilac
blossom, in early summer, this remaining open even when the sun has left it,
though it shuts in rain.

There is much self-sowing, in this garden, and none more so than by the
annual (but overwintering) *Omphalodes linifolia*, which flowers like a much
improved gypsophila and has glaucous foliage. *Sparaxis* have been long established. They are close relatives of ixias, the most usual colouring (all in the
same flower) being yellow, black and orange red. A delightful gladiolus, here,
that looks like a species, though it may not be, with zones of white and rosy
red. A *Beschorneria yuccoides* (sufficiently described elsewhere) was carrying a
7-foot long panicle, and a prickly wattle, *Acacia pravissima*, was behind and to
the left of this. It is of a jagged, hostile appearance, deep green but softened
when flowering in spring, with pouffs of yellow, scented blossom. It is one of
the hardier species worth trying in British gardens.

Convolvulus althaeoides was weaving around, so charming with its silvery
foliage and stems setting off pink convolvulus flowers but a bit of a devil, with
its spreading root system, when placed against plants that could be engulfed.
Still, I was rather ashamed of myself for getting rid of it and have brought it
back. 'I don't care,' was Helen Dillon's reaction to its behaviour with her.
There are early bulbs like *Scilla bifolia* around it, taking advantage of the
breathing space before the convolvulus gets into its stride.

So we crept up the garden, Beth always volubly in the lead. Your heartbeat
goes funny when you come upon a clump of the North American slipper
orchid, *Cypripedium reginae*, with its fat pink pouches, a dozen of them in
flower at a time, just at their freshest. No nursery lists that in *The Plant Finder*.
They'd lose their stock in five minutes, by fair means or foul, if the news got
around. There are columbines behind this and *Codonopsis clematidea*, just
opening its bells, in front. It is a flower that deserves to be raised, so as to
admire the geometrical design and colour zoning within, but the powerful
odour of fox need not be dwelt on. Making a 2-foot-tall plant at most, this is
easily raised from seed and will probably flower in its second year.

Many of Helen's celmisias originated from Beech Park, where David
Shackleton created another famous garden, just outside Dublin. The Irish and
Scottish climates suit these New Zealand alpine daisies, with their (usually)
silver-grey leaves, far better than the drier air and hotter sunshine of south-
east England. The one that was showiest when I visited, and that was grouped
prominently in a front of border position, was *Celmisia semicordata*, which may

Celmisia coriacea (possibly *C. semicordata*), a New Zealander with stiff, grey-green leaves.

be a synonym for the better-known name, *C. coriacea*, though the two have separate entries in *The Plant Finder*. Anyway, it has large, glistening white daisies above sparkling grey lance leaves. The sheen on these is comparable with an astelia's. The deep red club heads of *Persicaria millettii*, only 15 inches tall, grow in front of this. It flowers continuously for months, but never much at any one time.

Pimpinella major 'Rosea', an umbellifer, light and airy in habit, about 2½ feet tall, can vary a lot in the intensity of its pink flower colouring, from washed out to quite deep and rich. Needless to say, Helen has the most intensely coloured strain and it will generally self-sow in good shades, if it starts off good. That was in a lively grouping with the clean green and white variegation and sharp sword leaves of *Irish pallida* 'Argentea Variegata'; the white form of bloody cranesbill, *Geranium sanguineum* 'Album' (rather too thin and gappy a bloom, for my liking, but I'm trying what is reputed to be an improved form); a young, variegated *Weigela florida* (which may have to be found a roomier space); behind these, a glossy, green ivy on a wall and, in front of it, a white form of the fast-growing shrub mallow, *Abutilon vitifolium*. There's a rose bush, hereabouts, too. Roses are sensibly integrated with other plantings.

The hybrid, *A.* × *suntense*, between the last and *A. ochsenii*, was looking its best, with masses of deep lavender blossom, on the Dillons' boundary, so that over the wall top it was able to benefit from the background of their neighbour's dark cedar, in front of which is a large yellow-leaved shrub which I couldn't identify at a distance, though that didn't diminish its supporting role. Mauve against yellow, and darkness behind them, looks pretty good.

I can only, rather disjointedly, pick out plants and groupings from here and there. *Viola* 'Jackanapes', contrasting bronze above and brazen yellow beneath in an impudent, punchy little flower, is guaranteed to catch the eye. As is the way of violas, it had infiltrated an earlier flowering peony species, with finely dissected leaves, *Paeonia tenuifolia*.

I do like bold, look-at-*me* plants and such is *Astrantia major involucrata* 'Shaggy', so named by Margery Fish, who introduced it. The jagged bracts are prominent on its large, pale green inflorescences, and it was well suited by cardoon foliage for companionship. Then there were the drooping chestnut bells in an umbel on 3-foot stems of an ornamental onion, now called *Nectaroscordum siculum* (anyone but a botanist can see that it's an allium), that being mixed in with the yellow, black-flecked *Lilium pyrenaicum*. This lily, in a strong grouping, was also well paired with the scalloped heart leaves of *Macleaya macrocarpa*, the lily's being linear, in a long, dense column. The plume poppy is a terrible thug, of course, and its suckering habits are in perpetual need of controlling, but that's how gardening is. The plants are fighting it out

with each other and we are fighting it out with them, when we're not protecting them from strangulation. It's fight, fight, fight, but everything has to look totally relaxed. How little does the non-gardener guess.

Astrantia major spp. *involucrata* 'Shaggy' (a selection of Margery Fish's), with cardoon foliage.

Lilies appear to thrive. There was a huge colony on the garden's boundary of *Lilium henryi*; the eponymous Augustus Henry used to live on the neighbouring property. Though not yet flowering at the time of my visit, its colouring is soft apricot. There were also stray bulbs of the leopard lily, *L. pardalinum*, whose orange and red colouring Helen finds difficult (I don't), though an established colony, thanks to its rhizomatous roots, is not so easily got rid of.

We are, however, on safer and indisputably sublime territory when we come to a beautifully healthy colony of the double white sweet rocket, which looks like a stock that has learned the art of growing gracefully. When riddled with virus, this clone, which can only be propagated vegetatively, was a hopeless hospital case, but since it has been cleaned up (by micropropagation) it is a changed plant. I only wish these propagators, who are seldom plantsmen and haven't much cash to spare for unprofitable projects, would turn their attention to other virus-riddled plants, badly in need of cleansing: *Daphne odora* 'Aureomarginata', Malmaison carnations, *Hypericum* 'Hidcote' and *Narcissus* 'Tête-à-Tête', for instance.

I was much taken by a polygonatum, growing robustly into an upright, many-dark-stemmed clump, with numerous whorls of quite showy, mauve flowers and purplish linear leaves, also in whorls. This was *P. curvistylum*. When a plant is growing well, it looks deceptively easy. I am tempted, yet have an uneasy feeling that Dixter would not please it. I am not tempted by *Myosotidium hortensia*, the Chatham Islands forget-me-not, with great, cabbagy, deeply veined leaves and trusses of large, forget-me-not-like flowers, too heavy to stand erect and always recumbent. That was thriving in a shady border under a wall. It likes damp, cough-mixture air and needs a good deal of cosseting when it turns hot and dry.

Arisaemas and trilliums take advantage of shade in this garden; sanguinarias (Canadian bloodroot) and ferns. A lovely big patch of *Vancouveria chrysantha* (like epimedium, an esoteric member of the berberis family), with sprays of pale yellow blossom. Most of us only know (if we know any) *V. hexandra*, with rather too wee, white flowers.

This garden has so many delights and over so many seasons, that it obviously needs visiting over and over again. I wish I lived nearer. For the lucky ones who do, it is frequently opened.

Abroad

THE RUTH BANCROFT GARDEN

PROVIDED you love plants, there is no need to limit your excitement and interest in them to those which you can grow in your own garden. To find yourself in a completely different sphere to what you're used to is enormously stimulating, whether it be in Japan, Singapore or California. You bring to the scene your own training in the subject, and that helps, but you also need to modify and adjust your codes and prejudices. Then, if the experience is a good one, it is like living again. It is as though scales have fallen from your eyes and you can see everything in a new light.

The best gardens are a personal expression and this is very much the case with Ruth Bancroft's at Walnut Creek, not far from San Francisco. Mr Hubert Howe Bancroft bought the property in 1865. Ruth married into the family and arrived on the scene in 1939. Her husband, not unusually with males, thought that crop-producing plants were the only kind worth growing. Well, she does produce marvellous lemon drinks, for consumption following a garden tour in the cool shadow of her home, and the lemon that grows them is there before you, within friendly hailing distance.

Ruth Bancroft was interested in gardening for as long as she can remember (so were several others mentioned in this book – most of them perhaps) and she started in Berkeley, which is also in the Bay area but more temperate, sharing with San Francisco the almost daily fogs that come in from the ocean in the summer months. Walnut Creek is hotter in summer, colder in winter.

Her first succulent garden was quite a small affair within the confines of the total garden area, here, and she started that in the late 1960s. It grew and grew and is now the dominant theme. Other kinds of gardening are practised but they are less important because (my own interpretation, this) they cannot be performed with the same bold brush strokes that cacti, aloes, agaves, yuccas, phormiums, puyas, palms, aeoniums and their like (not all succulent by any means) lend themselves to.

But before going further in that direction I will here mention a splendid

A brilliant mixture of soft textures, with hard *Yucca filifera* backed by soft *Robinia pseudoacacia* 'Frisia'.

Agaves contribute to this garden of living sculpture.

planting of *Acanthus mollis*, a great wadge of them, just at their best in May–June, with cohorts of tall flower spikes rising from amid broadly scalloped foliage as relaxed as the inflorescence is stiff. Iris foliage was the foreground, while behind stood a magnificent palm (related to the date), *Phoenix canariensis*, whose leaves are 20 feet long but narrow and with scores of leaflets. To one side, scarlet flowers spangled a large bush of pomegranate.

Another planting (near to where cars park) that particularly impressed me on my first visit in 1986 (the second was on 1 June 1990) was a grove of the Mexican bamboo, *Arthrostylidium* (I can't find it in my books), carrying dense trusses of long, fine-spun leaves. The stout canes are sturdier than any we can grow in our climate but they were well thinned, so that you could look through this forest, and that is something we can and should emulate with any bamboo, except the very smallest. Within a garden setting, the Japanese wouldn't think of leaving their bamboos unthinned and they remove dead leaves as soon as they have fallen, or sooner. If we think that this is too much trouble, the loss is ours.

The main part of Ruth Bancroft's garden is furnished with the kinds of plants I listed above and which can be seen in my photographs. But photographs are two-dimensional and it is the third dimension of which you are, when in the middle of it, so intensely aware. For these are strong shapes and the sun provides them with strong shadows, both on to one another and against the pale ground.

This is a plant sculpture garden. As you move through it, shapes advance and recede and change their interrelationships. It becomes a mobile sculpture garden of the boldest design.

Your feeling of relaxation is largely thanks to the very wide gravel paths which merge, without dividing lines, into the plantings. You can't call them beds or borders. You are not aware of any overall design; rather of wonderful plant groupings. The one non-plant feature that really matters is a shelter – shelter from bad weather in winter and from excessive sunshine in summer. It is a kind of awning on stilts and it is shaped in an easy curve to form a crescent.

The shelter bed is called No. 6! No unnecessary pretensions there. But the contents are apt to escape. The *Agave alternata* leans outwards on its woody elbow; then makes another rosette of leaves and leans out a little further (some of my oldest ferns behave like this). When you look through these leaves, which have a double curve, against the sun, they are slightly translucent, despite their thickness. At their thin margins, the sea green changes to a rim of pale yellow. In front of you is their black shadow, a kind of *alter ego* lying on the floor with outstretched limbs.

Agave americana is the one we know best in Europe, together with 'Variegata', which has a broad central rich-cream-coloured band. The sinuous curves that these leaves take on would be called sexy in a human and it's easy to think of the plants in these terms.

Better than *A. americana* is *A. franzosinii*, which is on the largest scale and grows in a colony of its own, straight out of the dirt and without any special bed. Its leaves are gunmetal blue-grey. They wave and interlock in a stately ritual dance.

The long-quilled porcupine leaves of *Dasylirion longissimum*, narrow but quadrangular in section, are fairly flexible and describe a hemisphere wherein everything looks fresh, right down to ground level. Each plant is a single undivided unit and so these are widely spaced. They form a colony but of discrete units, which makes a good contrast to the groupies.

Were I an *habitué* of the French and Italian Rivieras, I should be familiar with *Yucca filifera*, but I am not. It is a strangely compelling plant, making a narrow column to 20 feet, generally unbranched as we were seeing it here, because it rarely flowers. What seems to be indefinite growth does, in suitable circumstances, come to a halt at flowering, subsequent to which the plant branches, and this it can do quite freely.

Y. filifera was here flatteringly set off by a tree of *Robinia pseudoacacia* 'Frisia' of the bright yellow leaves. In England, this popular plant of suburbia is more likely to be seen near a purple-leaved Norway maple.

Ruth Bancroft is clever at mixing stark material with trees or shrubs of

Yucca rostrata caught at its peak.

softer texture or outline. They go well with pines, for instance (she has the Mexican *Pinus montezumae*). Then a Mexican blue palm, *Butia armata*, with fans of long, narrow leaflets, is seen next to a rounded leguminous tree, *Parkinsonia aculeata*, which is a haze of pale green with tiny leaves. This has scented yellow flowers with an orange centre.

Most of the fiercer plants erupt into exciting blossom, from time to time. Agaves shoot up like a geyser. Yuccas start that way, then explode like a firework into a huge candelabrum of white bells. The puyas are most extraordinary of all. *Puya berteroniana* has a flowering stem as sturdy as a tree trunk. Each stiff unit in its panicle ends in a long, admonitory spine but is clothed along the way with bright green, silk-smooth, open-tubular flowers. Any flower of this shape, or with narrower tubes like the aloes, is visited by humming birds. I never overcame my feeling of childlike wonder each time I saw them darting from flower to flower. Then, suddenly exhausted, they would perch; the tiniest, fragile creatures.

In *Puya spathacea* the inflorescence is much slenderer and shorter, at a mere 4 feet, but widely branching, and it is the bright shrimp pink stems and bracts, more than the flowers, which draw the eye. These are bromeliads. If the condition were imposed on you that you could grow nothing but *Bromeliaceae* for the rest of your life, you could, given the right conditions, still be a happy gardener (although, as the majority are epiphytes, you'd have to be allowed *some* plants to grow them on).

Phormiums, New Zealand flax, look good here. There was a strongly upright-growing one to 6 feet with yellow striping that contrasted well with a young *Trachycarpus* palm whose leaves, held horizontally, clothed it down to ground level. There's something to be said for growing these as youngsters only and discarding them when they start to look woody (or woolly, seeing that they make a dense fibre) in their nether regions.

Cacti are largely represented by opuntias and I am glad I don't have to work near them. They are free with their satiny, rosette-shaped flowers around the rim of young pads. Ruth Bancroft still has to do a lot of the weeding among her plants. Hers was the first garden to be accepted by the Garden Conservancy scheme, which is to operate like our National Trust but for gardens only. She had hoped for some physical help from this, by now. With the garden being visited more and more, there is the need for greater input.

In a garden like this, what need of rose beds and herbaceous borders? But I liked a little garden where a range of pelargoniums, mostly the scented kinds, grows straight out of gravel. There are no beds, just gravel paths and pelargoniums between them. One called 'Toronto', with large pink flowers and aromatic foliage, appealed to me.

Left, opuntias predominate here. Many shapes build up this fascinating garden.

Right, the bromeliad *Puja spathacea* is pollinated by humming-birds.

And I was terribly envious of the way *Hunnemannia fumarifolia*, with its lacy blue foliage and yellow poppy flowers, grows and self-sows here. It makes strong, 2-foot-tall plants. I have to work at that one, a favourite annual.

My last word shall be with Amber, Ruth Bancroft's charming dog, which chases lizards and, although seven years old at the time, was still behaving like a puppy.

THE BORUN RESIDENCE

———◦———

IN JUNE 1994, Rosemary Verey and I combined on a three-week lecturing tour in the USA. We started in Los Angeles, and one of the first gardens we visited, on an agreeably hot, early summer's morning (3 June), was the Borun Residence. It wasn't long before I decided that this was a garden I should like to include as one of the last chapters written for my book. Luckily the owner, Ruth Borun, agreed to this.

The house, a single-storey building, was built in 1960 and Garrett Ecbo, a celebrated Californian landscape architect, visited the site before building commenced. Someone at his office, working from the house plans, then drew up the planting plan but without seeing the site. Most of the plants chosen were tropical. 'I don't want landscape architects; they don't know plants,' Ruth said to me.

She had three children to bring up and for years she did nothing about her dissatisfaction with the garden. Then she met Christine Rosmini and everything changed. Chris, who came into the picture in 1985 and has become a close friend, not only has an eye for design, which Ruth lacks – 'I don't have the vision,' she confessed – but she knows and loves plants, which is also Ruth's strength (she is a hands-on – or gloves-on – gardener). To get the most out of gardening, it is important to have a like-minded and equally committed friend or relation on whom to draw for ideas and off whom to bounce your own. This was not one of Ruth's husband's interests although, when all children were gone, he said, 'Now you can have the English garden you have always wanted,' and gave her a very generous cheque for her birthday, to use to build the garden of her dreams.

I saw quite a bit of Chris Rosmini on this visit; Rosemary was staying with her and the two of them came to the Borun Residence on that morning. Chris has a quiet strength which greatly impressed me. When in conversation with her, you don't for long scratch around the surface.

For a start, she weaned Ruth off the dominant expanses of lawn. She made

The Borun Residence with rose 'White Ice', centre.

terraces, for the house stands at the top of a slope. The terraces not only run in parallel with the house and its sitting-out area; they also curve round to the left so as eventually to run at right angles with the original line, here following the garden's boundary. The rather white 'stone' of which the terraces are built is composed of concrete slabs from a broken-up sidewalk. It doesn't jump at you.

There is a large oval pond at what appears, from the boundary beyond it, to be the bottom end of the garden, but the latter actually continues, heavily planted with trees, down a steep slope to a road. The only part of this that is seen from the house is the background of trees, and these continue, in an example of borrowed landscape, on to neighbours' territory. Some *Pinus thunbergii* have been carefully thinned and pruned at the Boruns' instigation.

Although the feel of the garden's central area is open, which suits many plants, shade is very necessary even in an English garden and far more so in the climate of Los Angeles. Some of the trees within this garden were strange to me but others were familiar. There was the corkscrew-stemmed willow,

Salix matsudana 'Tortuosa', eucalyptus, a couple of liquidambars. And the garden has a number of corners, each embracing a seat, that are shaded at various times in the day, so that you can choose where to be. Looking back to the house from below it, you are aware of a frieze of Washingtonia palms rising above its roof line. Tall and elegant, their long, naked trunks are crowned with a tuft of foliage. In many parts of suburban Los Angeles, they are combined effectively, sometimes lining the streets, with lower, sturdier, broad-crowned phoenix, relations of the date palm.

There is moving water at the top of this garden, alongside the principal sitting-out area with its enormous sunshade. How much, or whether it depends on a circulating pump, I do not know but the noise of water falling from pool to pool – three of them – is discreet, not meddlesome. The top pool has water-loving perennials emerging from it, while blue water-lilies flower well above the water level. *Canna glauca* and its hybrids, with narrow greyish foliage, are often seen in California as emergent aquatics but Ruth finds hers so invasive that it has to be confined to a pot.

The top water-lily pool, near the house. (You have to imagine the water-lilies to be blue!)

Nice features to hold your interest, around here. For instance, between two pools there is a large patch, in the paving, of a grey plant that hugs the ground like coarse grass. It is actually a composite, *Dyomdia margarettae*. Glazed, high-fired, hand-thrown pots, originally intended for bonsai, have various contents. They compose a little village. I was also taken by the combination, growing in the ground, of a self-sown fern, *Cyrtomium falcatum*, behind a white agapanthus. This evergreen fern, barely hardy and not nearly as lush as I should like it in my garden, has broadly sculpted, highly polished pinnae.

The borders created behind the terracing were filled with good, imported soil. Their contents are thoroughly mixed in just the way that I should choose to plant myself. Rose bushes are integrated in these plantings. Nowhere are they herded together. Most of those I saw in Los Angeles were already, in early June, a sorry mess – I was told I should have seen them a month earlier. But there were some charmers at the Borun residence. For instance, a prolific dwarf Polyantha called 'Green Ice'. 'Happenstance', smothered in single, cream yellow flowers was an obvious *Rosa bracteata* hybrid; in fact a seedling of 'Mermaid'. The soft yellow 'Graham Thomas' was growing next to what looked, to me, like a bush of smallish, highly decorative oranges. It is known as the Rangpur lime. In front were the bold purple rosettes of succulent *Aeonium arboreum* 'Atropurpureum', and beside that, a dark-centred, apricot-coloured day-lily.

Rose 'Graham Thomas', Rangpur lime (in fruit) and purple-leaved aeonium.

Ruth and her daughter, Nancy, enjoy shopping at the market together, for bedding plants and annuals. Those that we should consider tender perennials are not tender here at all. The lacy, grey-leaved *Tanacetum* (*Chrysanthemum*)

Tanacetum ptarmiciflorum with cup-and-saucer Canterbury bell behind and the variegated *Cornus florida* 'Welchii' (formerly 'Tricolor').

ptarmiciflorum, used in our public gardens as an edger, makes a large shrub here. It was with a purple, cup-and-saucer Canterbury bell and, behind them, the brightly variegated dogwood, *Cornus florida* 'Tricolor' (correctly 'Welchii'), which has a broad pink margin to the leaf and becomes extravagantly colourful before leaf fall.

Borun and Rosmini are strongly colour-conscious and like to organize harmonies within the same range. In a red situation, there was a plant of scarlet dianthus – probably 'Telstar Red' – in the centre of a hummock of the jazzy *Houttuynia cordata* 'Chameleon', with much of carmine in its variegated leaf. Near by, a crimson regal pelargonium. Over a terrace wall hung a curtain of a cherry red ivy-leaved pelargonium. Being hardy, here, these pelargoniums made impressive curtains and hummocky lumps over retaining walls.

Another perennial that we have to treat as tender is the lacy-leaved cranesbill, *Geranium incanum*, with magenta flowers. I grew it for a while but then forgot to take cuttings for overwintering under glass. That grew near to a pure white bedding lobelia (*Lobelia erinus*), while a mauve variety looked nice next to *Diascia* 'Ruby Field', which is a definite shade of pink without too much salmon included.

As in most gardens that I visit, there is a certain fear of, or antipathy towards, orange or bright yellow flowers. Thus a dazzling clump of perennial *Tagetes limonii*, with single flowers resembling a coreopsis, was excused by Chris on the grounds that it normally flowered early, when there was little colour in the garden, but had this year continued later than scheduled. It has rich green, finely cut leaves with a strong aroma and was sited behind a

An overwintered ivy-leaved pelargonium.

flowering group of quaking grass, *Briza maxima*. Excuses were unnecessary, I felt, though not unexpected.

I should mention that borders are heavily mulched with bark and that irrigation, essential in this sort of garden, is laid on throughout, since there is virtually no rainfall in summer and early autumn. It is used, in the growing season, three times a week.

At the top of one of the garden's boundaries, close to the house, the dividing fence has a narrow border of black-stemmed bamboo (*Phyllostachys*) and a solid path in front of it. So its questing rhizomes are safely contained. This is far more difficult to ensure in a warm climate, where bamboos are so much more vigorous and invasive than with us. *Phyllostachys* is a pretty polite genus in most of Britain.

Lower down this boundary is an informal hedge of privet, *Ligustrum japonicum*, flowering and scented on the air at the time of my visit. In front of it an old-fashioned, Grandiflora type of red sweet pea, whose season would be brief but none the less welcome. Because of their extra heavy scent, these are the only sweet peas that I grow. Their season, in a hot climate, is short. At a low level, it was mingling with a modern, mauve-flowered alstroemeria.

I always seem to be in California just when the Australian kangaroo paws, *Anigozanthos*, are at their best and there are some wonderful hybrids. The weirdly shaped, furry flowers, here in shades of bronze and deep burnt orange, are crowded towards the branching top of 6-foot-tall, naked stems. As with so many flowers, it is better to visit them where they grow happily than to attempt them ourselves. Envy is out of place.

Modern alstroemeria and old-fashioned, highly scented sweet pea.

One of the plants I enjoyed most in Ruth's garden – and I don't remember seeing it before – was the shrubby *Salvia canariensis*. Its habit is similar to *S. interrupta*, which we can grow in the warmer parts of England. That is to say, it makes a lowish, grey-leaved shrub, but the flowering stems rise way above, to 6 feet and more. In this case, flowers, calyxes and bracts are all strongly on the pink side of mauve. There was a good deal of this, with a clump of opium poppy seed-heads near by and a huge clump of miscanthus, the Japanese grass which flowers much later but makes a bold feature with its foliage, early on.

As you would expect of its humanitarian owner, plants are allowed to seed themselves around, so furry verbascum leaf rosettes sit complacently in a gravel path. There was much of the inestimable *Verbena bonariensis*, whose clustered heads of light purple blossom, held high on almost leafless stems, keep on and on from an early summer start. It is a strongly three-dimensional plant, 'floating in mid-air', to quote Chris Rosmini.

All that I have so far described unfolds from the garden front of the house. There is, however, more garden between the house entrance and the wide gate through which you drive to reach it. There were two familiar plants that I could scarcely believe to see in full bloom so early. In England, quite apart from the necessity to treat it as a tender perennial, planted out in spring, you'll be lucky to have *Leonotis leonurus* (now *L. ocymifolia*) flowering before the end of our growing season in October. This tall labiate proudly carries upright ropes of orange-brown flowers in whorls, rather like a phlomis but in longer chains. An exciting plant.

Then, against a fence, there was a whole border of the shrubby *Salvia leucantha*, with felted grey leaves, grey flowering stems and silvery calyxes, but lavender blue flowers. This is arguably the most beautiful of all the sages, and there is plenty of competition. I have recorded (see page 113) that at Powis Castle the great skill of Jimmy Hancock has it flowering by July, but more normally it seldom gets going till September, in English gardens. Again, the plants need overwintering under frost-free glass.

Near to the house wall, there is an imposing, weathered rock. Chris discovered it in a stone yard. A hollow in its upper surface is kept filled with water for the birds to bathe in. And Chris introduced *Mahonia nevinii*, which grows near by and is a Californian native. Of delicate habit, its grey leaves, divided into five pinnae, are quite tiny. Yellow flowers are borne in winter and its tiny fruits turn orange.

With the pale wall as a background, I like the treatment of *Nandina domestica*, a Chinese shrub that we can treat as hardy in Britain but which seldom grows enthusiastically, whereas, where the summers are warmer, as in Japan and California, growth is exuberant and the panicles of white blossom are followed by spectacular red berries. Yet the habit of the shrub is its most attractive feature, with its loose rosettes of foliage, the leaves quite large, but intricately pinnate, each pinna narrow, giving a bamboo-like impression. Ruth prunes this carefully, so that each stem is bare up to its crown of whorled leaves. These crowns, seen in silhouette, are at different levels, since the stems are of different lengths.

A single morning is far too short to spend in such a place, but it gave me a taste. Gardens like this do not just happen; much thought and much work go into their creation and maintenance. But they convey a sense of achievement and a feeling of peace. Only nice people can bring this about.

NORTH HILL

—⇒•◦•⇐—

IN SOUTHERN Vermont, New England, is Wayne Winterrowd's and Joe Eck's garden at North Hill. It is the coldest garden in this book – coldest in winter, that is, but spells in July and August are frequently hot and sticky, for theirs is a continental climate. Winter temperatures can drop to minus 29°C (minus 20°F), yet their latitude around 43° north would, in Europe, place you somewhere between Florence and Rome.

Having stated the worst, there are mitigations. The garden is on a south-facing slope and cold air drains off it, making temperatures in the valley below considerably lower, during frosty weather. The altitude is 1,800 feet and the hills around tend to rise to ridges (rather than peaks) at some 3,000 feet. All is forest – secondary forest, as the original trees were felled by early settlers. Then, as they found better land for cultivation further west, they were allowed to grow again. Dominant trees in this forest are the American beech, *Fagus grandifolia*, and the sugar maple, *Acer saccharum*.

Fall colour is famed in Vermont, but why anyone should actually choose to live year round in these parts is a little puzzling. Perhaps it is good for Wayne's and Joe's garden design business. Or perhaps they had a belligerent desire to show the world what could be done with a garden in unpromising circumstances – they have to be entirely surrounded, in winter, with a prison-like palisade, to prevent deer from eating everything that remains visible above 5-foot-deep snow. Should the snow be subjected to a freak midwinter melt, all those plants that depend on being protected by its coverlet will be extinguished by frost.

There is a stream running right through the garden and this, combined with the favourable aspect, led to Wayne and Joe buying the site and building on it. That all started in 1976. There is a big kitchen-cum-dining-room with a large hearth (we were grateful for a fire, when the weather turned miserable, on the longest day of the year) and a brick floor. Wayne walks barefoot on this; he has beautiful toes. There is a delightful little red-flowered orchid (with

a name as long as my arm, ending in 'China Doll') on the kitchen windowsill. The flowers are borne in threes on 6-inch stems. The plant is tough and has survived temperatures down to freezing. This kitchen sink window looks out upon a conservatory, which runs alongside its outer wall. It is kept entirely unheated and fully ventilated, in summer, really coming into its own when such shrubs as camellias, leptospermum and tender rhododendrons bloom in spring. Beyond the conservatory is a flat, paved area where pots are stood about.

Pot culture features strongly in this set-up, allowing a big range of tender plants to be given a summer airing and the illusion, which all gardeners in 'cool' temperate climates crave, that (for a few weeks anyway) we're really living in semi-tropical conditions. There was a blue agapanthus in prodigious flower and a rich reddish purple petunia. Also a 'geranium' that strongly took my fancy, *Pelargonium* 'Vancouver Centennial', having red flowers and purple leaves with a pale margin.

On my first evening here (Rosemary Verey and I, driven from Boston by Tom Cooper, editor of *Horticulture*, having arrived soon after 4 p.m.), the weather was idyllic, with fleecy white clouds in a predominantly blue sky. I

The pond and bog at the bottom of the rock garden, with candelabra primulas in an uninhibited colour mix. *Iris laevigata* 'Variegata' flowering beyond.

Purple petunia in a pot near the back entrance.

was anxious to see and photograph as much as I could, while these conditions lasted. I had been warned of the fickleness of the climate. Rainfall is spread evenly and generously throughout the growing season. Next day proved wet, overcast and gloomy.

But in a garden so full of detail as this, no plantsman can progress even as fast as a snail. Early on, I was aware of an alley with large rose bushes just coming into their high season (no Los Angeles, this) and fat clumps of such well-loved double peonies as the soft pink 'Sarah Bernhardt' and white 'Festiva Maxima', with characteristic blood-red flecks spattered in its snow; a sharp, invigorating peony scent, too. Roses need to be ultra-hardy to be worth attempting. Prominent is a Canada-bred series, named after tough explorers. Few are repeat-flowering. Neither is 'Cardinal Richelieu', the mauve-purple colour of dusty grapes. The excellent *Rosa rugosa* 'Alba' does repeat, unless allowed to fruit, which is just as spectacular and takes up most of the shrub's energies. Neither this nor the other roses nor, indeed, other flowering shrubs generally – there was a vast *Kolkwitzia amabilis* near the roadside – appeared to sustain any pruning, 'romantic exuberance' being the preferred motto. Besides, during winters of deepest snow, deer can walk over the top of the defensive fence and do all the pruning for you, like it or not. Roses are among their choicest flavours.

The Perennial Garden runs alongside the rose–peony alley and I spent all the available time here, before enjoying the delicious meal prepared by Wayne. He has only one, self-confessed, weakness. 'I grow things beautifully,' he said, 'and I cook like an angel but I can't retain plant names. Joe will know.' This

Peony 'Sarah Bernhardt' in an area concentrating on hardy shrub roses.

in answer to one of my frequent inquiries: 'What is it?' The Perennial Garden includes the one hint of formality to be found at North Hill. The slope has been taken up by small limestone-stepped terraces. Removal of soil from one end to the other was all done in buckets, by hand. Wayne has not forgotten the experience.

Pots stand on these ledges. I was taken by a petunia of cascading habit, with small, light magenta, black-centred flowers, *P. integrifolia*. It is propagated from cuttings. Having seen it for the first time here, I then spotted it on several occasions back home. So often the way. *Solanum rantonnetii*, now reclassified as *Lycianthes*, though quite obviously a solanum to anyone but a botanist, has purple lampshade flowers all summer. This is planted out but cut back hard and repotted in the autumn. It is difficult, in England, to provide it with enough summer heat to flower it really freely. *Salvia confertiflora*, a lush, semi-woody perennial, with long, narrow spikes of small red flowers, had recently been planted out and was already flowering. With us it seldom gets going before September. *Salvia* 'Indigo Spires' was new to me and is half *S. farinacea*. Two-foot-tall plants of annual *Ammi majus*, delicate, purest white umbellifer, float through all the borders. Wayne and Joe do not have the space for raising annuals under glass, so this task is contracted out.

There was a grand spring display of black ('Queen of the Night') and white ('Maureen') tulips, these being hardy and long-lived if planted deep. They are followed by black and white seed strains of *Papaver somniferum*, grown separately, then put together.

I asked about how the borders were fed. They have a granular fertilizer in the ratio of 5 nitrate: 10 phosphate: 10 potash (the soil being deficient in these last two). And there is now manure from their own Highland cattle (very hardy; they stay out all winter), mixed with hay, leaves and suchlike to open its texture.

Box hedging is a feature that you expect in New England gardens, where (perhaps because exacting) it is extremely popular and there is a boxwood society. The hedges and specimens need to be encased by wooden crates or shutters in winter. Yew hedging grows well – that was a surprise – but is hand-trimmed with secateurs.

Next morning, after finding plenty of excuses for staying indoors till as late as was decent, we visited, from the front of the house (but it is the back door that is almost invariably used except on state occasions), the lower side of the garden. The Front Border, shaded by trees and shrubs, has a large concentration of hostas, with contributions from astilbes and *Kirengeshoma palmata*, the latter having handsome maple-like leaves, black stems and pale yellow shuttlecock flowers in late summer. With its pale, chartreuse green colouring, *Hosta* 'Zounds' has a consumptive appearance.

Downhill is an area concentrating on conifers but by no means on them alone. I liked *Picea mariana* 'Fastigiata'. A golden elm, *Ulmus* × *viminalis* 'Aurea', looked lush, with big leaves. Instead of the usual *Salix caprea* 'Kilmarnock' willow, which is male and dismally weeping, we saw the female 'Weeping Sally', which has fatter (though not yellow-powdered) pussies. Wayne prunes this to develop a wider-canopied umbrella habit. Conifers are interplanted with heathers and colchicums. 'You should see the heathers in August,' I was told. 'But I'm on the grouse moors in August. There's a bit of heather there,' from me, patently a lie. The heathers are protected by snow from destruction by frost. What a pity. The cone-shaped *Picea glauca* 'Sander's Blue' was enviably healthy; no trouble from red spider mite here. *Clematis koreana* flowers in flushes and was described as 'subtle' – an adjective of which I have learned to be suspicious when applied to flowers and plants. The colouring is a combination of muted purple and dingy straw. I remarked of a penstemon that I disliked its indeterminate colouring, neither purple nor blue. 'Oh,' Joe quickly leaped in, 'but that's the whole idea of all our planting. We call this the bruised garden.'

The conifer bed leads to the steeply falling rock garden; steep in part because a lot of bulldozed excavation was thrown up the bank in order to make a flat area of lawn and for the greenhouse at the bottom.

This rock bank is one of the most successful of its kind that I have seen, the rock well bedded in, well weathered, pleasing without being intrusive. It is granite excavated quite a few years ago from a site fairly close at hand, required for building, a nuisance to the builders and just left on the surface to one side, where it weathered. Joe and Wayne marked with a white cross the pieces they fancied, after which transport and relocation were the only expenses.

Rock features in England tend to reach a peak in April. Here, June was evidently the high spot. Masses of grey-leaved dianthus cushions covered with scented blossom, horned poppies (*Glaucium*), which self-sow, campanulas, including the nearly related edraianthus, stonecrop (*Sedum acre*), with rather paler yellow flowers than I remember them at home, *Salvia argentea*, flowering. The whole area has a nice open feel.

At the bottom of this bank, a pool and boggy area. The excavations had brought water gushing out of the hillside and, the parent rock being clay, this is held in any hollow without need of pond lining to retain it. At the time of our visit, there was a gaudy display of candelabra primulas in orange, apricot, brick, pink, puce, mauve – you name it. A complete freedom from subtlety. 'This is the vulgar section of the garden,' Wayne told me. As a contrast to five months of snow, something like it is needed. There was a swallowtail butterfly feeding on a primula, which I tried to photograph.

The boggy bits were well used. There was the so-called flowering rush, *Butomus umbellatus* with umbels of pink flowers crowning naked stems; the variegated sweet flag, *Acorus calamus* 'Variegatus', making a bold patch; an even stronger green and pure white variegation from *Iris laevigata* 'Variegata', covered in purple bloom; another highly variable iris, *I. virginiana*, in a good form, collected by Wayne.

Salvia argentea flowering with dianthus (sweetly scented pinks) on the rock bank.

An elegant hybrid derived from *Canna glauca*, flowering in the greenhouse.

All this is very near to the important greenhouse for overwintering stock, to which a potting and tool shed is the continuation. Along the outside wall of the latter is a raised, dry wall bed, packed 4 feet deep with 'bank run', which is gravelly trash left after a new road has been built. It is poor in nitrogen but rich in minerals, admirably suiting some otherwise tricky plants, like *Daphne arbuscula*. A raised bed of this kind brings small plants close to eye level, allowing them to be studied – and smelled – in comfort.

The greenhouse is double-glazed and heated remarkably economically with propane gas, a flue taking residues harmlessly into the open. It was this summer being used for a display of cannas, and a brave show they were making.

Taking a slightly different route, you can return uphill through the rhododendron garden, largely stocked with the ultra-hardy hybrids bred for a cold climate by Dr David Leach, who lives in Ohio. The hardier the hybrid, the duller its foliage. Luckily the plants are still on the small side and there is room for much else – to me of greater interest.

Aralia cachemirica was growing far more exuberantly than with me. It is a splendid perennial, 8 feet high or more when suited, and with bold pinnate foliage. The compound inflorescence consists of ivy-like flower umbels which turn purple as the berries ripen to near black. There was an exciting looking eupatorium, *E. altissimum*, already 10 feet high and bearing pale green leaves architecturally, in whorls. One thing to note about this garden is that it contains many plants of strong personality and design, which makes hard landscaping largely superfluous.

From here on, for the rest of the year and even in England, I have been bumping into a fast-growing, autumn-flowering shrub, *Heptacodium jasminoides*. Its opposite, ovate leaves remind me of a dogwood's. The scented blossom is borne in panicles, terminally, on young wood. Since it can be flowered reasonably early in autumn, at least in the south of England, I don't know why this isn't more grown. It isn't as though there is a plethora of flowering shrubs at that time of year. On a smaller scale, I also saw, for the first time, the purple-leaved form of *Lysimachia ciliata*, but have since acquired it for myself. The dark foliage highlights the yellow flowers so much better than does green. It is a quite low-growing perennial that increases rapidly by rhizomes, so I shall soon be replacing the type plant completely.

You come to a new bridge across the stream (there are two others, one of them made by 'a massive slab of field stone', to quote Wayne's own description), leading to a platform from which a *Gunnera manicata* planting will soon be the dominant feature. Gunneras are ridiculously tender for this climate; hence the challenge, for they are magnificent foliage plants. Four square holes have been excavated and lined with wooden shuttering. This will allow the plants to be set deep, for protection and to be covered with insulated plywood lids in winter. But why not emigrate?

As you wind your way upwards, across and across the bridges, many good plants are passed, with space for all but without overdoing any one group. The water saxifrage, *Darmera peltata*, is native to the Pacific coast states but is here thoroughly at home, self-sowing. There's an excellent group of blue poppies, *Meconopsis betonicifolia*, in a good perennial clone that makes multiple crowns. *Mertensia sibirica* attracted me, an 18-inch-tall, clump-forming plant carrying light blue, tubular flowers. It seemed happy in light shade. Canadian bloodroot, *Sanguinaria canadensis*, is very much at home, *Lilium canadense* naturalizes by self-sowing, and the pure white *Anemone canadensis* makes a colony. There is a *Hemerocallis altissima* hybrid with white flowers (I was too early for them) that open and exhale their scent at night.

In a plantsman's garden like this, so much takes the eye that it is difficult to know where to stop the descriptions. What about *Abies koreana* in a prostrate form, for instance, covering a wide area and coning only a little above ground level – a community of cones?

At the top of the garden, and separated from the rest, is a fenced-in, rectangular vegetable garden, formally laid out and beautifully kept. The crisscross of paths is surfaced with hay which remains weed-free thanks to an invisible bottom layer of newspaper, magazines and plant catalogues. All the vegetables and fruit (there were standard gooseberries and red currants; black currants are not popular) were thriving except for broad beans. All of this is most important to a dedicated chef. Wayne and Joe do employ quite a bit of help. They'd be tied hand and foot otherwise, and the garden doesn't seem to have stopped expanding.

Like all the best gardens, North Hill is highly individual and is always changing and developing. That makes it exciting, both for them and for those who are lucky enough to visit it. What are they up to now? must be the query before each successive visit. I shall hope to get back.

AYRLIES

———⊷⊙⊷———

I RARELY look at a garden without making notes. This is from habit and because I know that a note may somehow be useful at a later date, especially if it is of a plant unfamiliar to me – perhaps one that I should like to grow myself. But if I know that there is a probability or possibility of writing that garden up, because I like it and believe it to deserve wider recognition – sometimes because I have been asked to write about it – then my observation becomes much more intense, the notes and photographs far more numerous.

It was on my second visit to Ayrlies that I realized that I definitely wanted to include it in this book, and then not at the start of that visit but as I soaked myself in its ambience, for it is a garden which reveals itself and the vision of its owner gradually. The more I saw of it the more I enjoyed it.

A garden, of course, is an expression of its owner and she is very special – but this is not a biography. Malcolm and Beverley McConnell have been living at Ayrlies for some thirty years. He is no gardener but he is a great backer-up. Beverley loves to work on a large canvas. She keeps on thinking of more projects and of the greater expansion that will enable them. Many uncommitted husbands would groan. What do you want more for? they'd ask. Haven't you more than enough already? And a great deal along those lines. Greater expense, more labour, we're not getting any younger, you'll kill yourself … and all that. Instead of which, when the latest brainwave is outlined, 'Why not?' is Malcolm's encouraging reaction. (He is a construction engineer and there seems to be money around.) So she goes ahead.

I must say that this all-things-are-possible attitude is something you meet most frequently in countries of a progressive and pioneering outlook. Ayrlies is in New Zealand, not far from Auckland and overlooking the same Hauraki gulf, with a view out to the cone-shaped volcanic island of Rangitota. From the air, the countryside seems to be divided into small fields and woods, very much in the English style, but as soon as you're down to earth and see the

The stag's-horn fern, *Platycerium bifurcatum*, on a willow trunk.

woods filled with exotica like tree ferns, you realize that the climate is warm and wet.

Annual rainfall at Ayrlies is 52 inches, though it is dry enough in January and February for the extensive lawns to suffer. There is irrigation. Lichens grow on all surfaces, with the air being so moist. On garden seats, for instance, and on all trees, however vigorously they may be growing. Most are grey but some are bright ochre yellow. No birch can have a silver trunk. Unless washed annually, the bark is overlaid. Better not to grow birches, as Beverley is rapidly concluding.

But growth is tremendously fast compared with what we are used to. Everything was planted by her (*qui facet per alium, facet per se*). Eucalypts are 80 feet tall. A pin oak, *Quercus palustris*, is 60 feet and still in the full vigour of youth. Many liquidambars have been planted at various times and they have reached up to 40 feet. Do they colour well? I asked, and are they seedlings or known clones selected for reliable autumn colouring and propagated vegetatively? They are seedlings, but the nurseryman who raised them took his seed from trees having the best colour and the progeny do, in fact, perform well.

The garden is by no means overtreed, but there is 10 acres of it, so trees are needed. Especially in a warm climate, you are looking for shade and so are many plants. One of the most striking is the Norfolk Island pine (not a pine at all), *Araucaria excelsa*, which I think looks its best when all its branches are retained, so that the lowest sweep the ground. I often saw this tree in Australia, but it always looked scruffy after a few years. Here it is truly at home and grows at a great rate. So starkly formal in outline and dark in colouring that some folks find it forbidding or overpowering. I relish it.

There are four ponds (the clay soil retains water without need of lining), and swamp cypresses, *Taxodium distichum*, thrive at the water's edge, their weird knee roots adept at retaining the bank. Weeping willows do well, at least for a time, and the fascinating stag's-horn fern, *Platycerium bifurcatum*, was growing on the trunk of one of these.

Three trees were flowering notably on my visit in early December, all of them sweetly scented. An elegant specimen of the evergreen, pittosporum-related *Hymenosporum flavum* smells strongest at night. *Melia azederach*, a gaunt deciduous tree with pinnate leaves, has panicles of small mauve star flowers smelling deliciously of chocolate. One of these is strategically planted by a sitting-out terrace. *Rhus succedanea*, another deciduous tree with pinnate leaves, was alive with bees foraging among its panicles of lime green blossom, very sweet on the air.

The garden lies on a quite steep slope – north-facing, I should say, as it

The compelling formality of a
Norfolk Island pine, *Araucaria
excelsa*.

receives plentiful sunshine (and we are in the southern hemisphere). The rock
garden is truly matured, being full of self-sowers, most of which are bulbs or
corms. They were at their best on my first visit, in late September, notably
ixias, sparaxis and babianas – the last like chunkier versions of ixias and mainly
purplish in colouring. Sparaxis are typically bronze with a yellow throat, the
flower being funnel-shaped. One shouldn't envy gardeners who can grow

Bronze sparaxis and self-sowing cinerarias beneath a lemon.

plants that we can't, or think we can't, but sometimes can. The books have deceived us. You don't have to believe them when they say that something is suitable for the greenhouse. So it may be, but given a warm spot it may also be hardy in the garden. First I found that ixias were, in mine; then sparaxis, and next I shall try babianas. I shan't expect them to seed around but if they'll just look happy I shall be well content.

These things were mixed in with familiars like *Alyssum saxatile, Convolvulus cneorum*, pansies and violas, hoop petticoat daffodils and *Narcissus juncifolius*. Huge carpets of gazanias, which are hardy here, were already blooming in September and at their peak in December. Doubtless they would continue untiringly for several months yet. Most were yellow, the double variety we call 'Yellow Buttons' notably good. In fact they form part of an area where Beverley concentrates yellow plants, including a low, shrubby conifer, which one would call golden. Through this weaves an excellent indigo, *Indigofera australis*, a suckering sub-shrub with spikes of substantial light pink pea flowers. The pink and the yellow contrast well. That was in December. By then the above-mentioned bulbs were being cut down and cleared, but an elegant habranthus, *H. robustus*, with heads of pink amaryllis-like funnels, was flowering and that self-sows. An iridaceous flower then at its best was the pale yellow, 4-foot tall *Moraea ramosissima*. This has a graceful, open habit and the flowers open at midday. I bet some of us could be growing it in our English gardens.

Ayrlies' lawns are occasionally interrupted, by way of welcome variety, by setting wooden sleeper steps (all steps in this garden are wooden) into the slope, thus forming a platform on which to place a seat. The step crannies are

Gazania 'Yellow Buttons' mixed with pink *Indigofera australis*.

Wooden sleeper steps making a platform in the lawn. Growing in them, bright green *Scleranthus biflorus*, daisies (*Erigeron karvinskianus*): a golden planting across the lawn.

planted with such as *Erigeron karvinskianus* (predictably ebullient, its daisies changing from white, on opening, to pink); a very tight, bright green, cushion-forming plant, *Scleranthus biflorus*, and *Viola hederacea*, a charming Australian species of violet in white and indigo, which I call the chinless wonder, as its lowest petals recede. Another excellent step-cracks plant, both here and elsewhere, and one that I intend to try myself, is *Nierembergia rivularis* (now *N. repens*). Keeping very low, it creeps along any fissure and expands its quite large, white moon flowers when the sun has warmed it up.

The rose garden is by no means dominated by roses. Beverley appreciates that they need companions and many of these are annuals or self-sowing perennials. *Echium plantagineum* 'Blue Bedder' was there (the Patterson's Curse of Victoria and New South Wales, where it has become a weed of vast acreages of disturbed land); the bright pink mallow, *Lavatera trimestris* 'Loveliness'; the white form of *Lychnis coronaria*; a creamy white eschscholtzia of great charm, this growing next to one of the modern German-bred yarrows, 'Salmon Beauty'. I find its colouring, as others of this origin, grubby and indeterminate, but Beverley likes the change in colour between new and old flowers.

Two of David Austin's roses were outstanding. 'Leander' makes a big shrub (in this climate, anyway) carrying pale peach-coloured, flat and very double

Rose 'Graham Thomas' treated as a climber.

flowers in a big truss. It has a long season and doesn't go mouldy in wet weather, contrary to what might be expected in so full a bloom. The soft yellow 'Graham Thomas' was here treated as a climber to 6 or 7 feet against a fence, and this is clearly the most satisfactory way with it. As a bush, it throws long canes during the current season, bearing such a heavy truss of blossom at their summit that the whole lot sway over to the ground.

Of 'Bloomfield Abundance', the miniature rose on a large shrub that is so often passed off by nurseries as 'Cécile Brunner', Beverley said it never gave her the right feeling. 'It looks as though it's been eaten by a possum,' with its long, stringy, unfurnished inflorescence.

This is in the oldest part of the garden. 'We've got to get the wheelbarrow waltz going a bit here,' Beverley observed of things that needed throwing out. Of *Sisyrinchium striatum* she wisely remarked that it's best as an annual. Then its 18-inch spikes of pale yellow flowers are seen in a setting of clean sword leaves. On old plants, much derelict, blackened foliage becomes evident. Many modern day lilies, hereabouts, some more stylish than others. Their name is legion. One called 'Memories', apricot shading to burnt orange and with rippled margins, stood well over 3 feet and rested its chin coyly over the back of a seat. 'Happy Reward' was another good one, pale yellow shading to rose buff at the tips; slightly frilly and excellently scented. That counts for a lot in a day lily. But there are now so many cultivars and their naming is such an industry in America, that nurseries can only hope to stock a tiny fraction of them. Neither of the above two seems to have reached Britain and I dare say we're not much the poorer.

Steep wooden steps lead down through the rose garden to the most cherished of the four ponds. What a difference water makes to a garden and what glamorous plants there are that enjoy watery conditions.

In the pond itself is a crimson nymphaea; a yellow one, 'Chromatella', which is an old favourite in England; and, flowering later, a blue tropical variety. Apart from the excitement of being able to grow a blue water-lily at all, their blooms are held well above the water's surface, unlike the hardy kinds, and that does lend them a presence. A sumptuous display, when I was there, of *Iris kaempferi* (now *I. ensata*) cultivars, so voluptuous with their broad, silken falls.

Calla lilies, which we would call arums (forms of *Zantedeschia*), are a feature around the ponds in this garden. In a garden setting, the spathes of 'Green Goddess', though good in flower arrangements, blend only too successfully with its bold leaves. But clones vary; some are whiter than others and there is a good deal of white in the Ayrlies examples. I may say that straight *Zantedeschia aethiopica* is a naturalized weed along all stream banks, in this part of the world, making a wonderful display in spring, but sourly regarded by the farmers. Unlike Cleopatra, custom can stale.

Thanks to recent hybridization, there now seems to be infinite variety in arum lilies. They come in many colours; mahogany red, burnt orange and intense yellow are all well represented at Ayrlies, among attractively white-speckled foliage and on dwarf plants. They can appear too dwarf, a little stumpy, in fact, but not if well fed, well established and well watered.

There is a large, newish planting of dwarf, evergreen Kurume azaleas on

Iris kaempferi by the willow pond.

the bank leading back to the house (which is a low, rambling affair) and they will undoubtedly improve in time as they develop more shape and individuality. My criticism of this type of azalea is that it makes such dense blobs of uncompromising colour. Among them, spring-flowering cinerarias, of the kind we grow in pots for conservatory display, are naturalized and self-sow. Some of *their* colours are pretty violent and apt to quarrel with the azaleas. At other times, they seed themselves in just the right place, as where a magenta cineraria was growing beneath the pendent fruits of a lemon bush, its branches coming down to the ground. Sparaxis were mixed in with this (in late September).

The beautiful but subtropical Vireya rhododendrons can be grown comfortably outside in these parts, and Beverley has a project to make a big planting of these together with ferns, which should fulfil the role of masking the shrubs' naturally stemmy habit. Really, these rhododendrons are epiphytes, so perhaps she should be building huge, rotting wood piles into which to plant the rhodos, so that they could hang out of and down from them. Now there's a project!

The stem of the pin oak on the bank leading back to the house has been well trimmed up so as to allow generous plantings beneath it of shade-lovers. These are much as we should use them in Britain. A bright green, large-leaved hosta is clearly a close derivative of *H. plantaginea*. *Dicentra formosa* 'Alba' not only has white flowers but shows its albino nature in the pale green colouring of its leaves. *Iris foetidissima* is represented in its variegated form. Bowles's golden grass, *Milium effusum* 'Aureum', always looks brightest in spring and in light shade. *Asplenium bulbiferum*, an evergreen fern, tender with us, makes masses of small, putative young plants on top of its fronds. Its dark tone contrasts with lighter plantings. Of the creeping *Saxifraga stolonifera*, there is a big carpet. This is charming both for its stripy shell leaves and for its airy panicles of pale, lopsided blossom in early summer. Near by, both blue and white lacecap hydrangeas were already flowering well before the longest day.

Elsewhere, another shade-lover (at least in this climate), the foot-tall, poppy-related *Eomecon chionanthum*, whose rhizomatous habit quickly extends its range, was covered with white blossom amid rounded, glaucous foliage. It is a good doer in Britain, but shy-flowering. Clivias flower abundantly in spring and are happy in shade. Their cultivation offers no problems except for miserable inroads on their old, evergreen foliage by slugs and snails. *Strelitzia reginae*, the bird of paradise flower, with beak-like flowers in orange and pale blue, can be similarly affected. This is a moisture-lover for the pondside and it was quaint to see it with blue water forget-me-nots for companionship. Close to the house, beneath a melia tree, is a colony of busy lizzies, *Impatiens* hybrids, which has been going for twenty years. It is shorn hard back each winter.

A number of climbers, against the house and on fences and other buildings, took my fancy. The heavily scented, early spring-flowering *Jasminum polyanthum* is much more definitely pink in bud than we see it as a cool greenhouse plant. It gets a hard cut-back immediately after flowering. The abundance of white, tubular blossom on spring-flowering *Pandorea pandorana* (a relative of *Campsis* and *Catalpa*), makes a strong impression on anyone new to it, as I was. *Petraea volubilis* I knew from my student days, as a climber for the Intermediate House. Its fresh-looking panicles of star-shaped blossom consist of rich, velvety purple corollas and more persistent, lighter mauve calices framing them. It flowers against the house wall in two flushes. Bougainvillaea, alongside it, is in a deep red form, which seems to be the most popular colour in these parts (my sneaking affection remains with the brightest magenta possible). It creates a warm red glow in the room behind it. A little further along is *Solanum wendlandii*, with large mauve potato flowers. On a summerhouse near the swimming-pool is a wonderful mix, quite early in the season, of the long mauve tresses of *Wisteria floribunda* with a coral pink climbing rose – probably one of those varieties popular on the Riviera which are not hardy enough with us in Britain. I am trying to think of any similar but hardy climbing rose that would already be flowering in time to coincide with wisterias in England.

I have concentrated on what is the core of the garden, but much is happening nearer its boundaries. For instance, a steep bank leading down to the boundary fence, which Beverley has colonized with seedlings of *Echium pininana*, which I describe as such a feature in the Ventnor Botanic Garden (see pages 8–9). Its thick columns of blue flowers (of which there are more next to the house) rise to 10 feet or so and, once established, self-seeding is the order of the day. These are mixed in with another monocarpic plant, *Geranium maderense*, biggest and boldest of the tribe, its magenta flowers coinciding with the echium's early summer season.

It is so good to think that this garden, after thirty years, is still developing as creatively as ever; developing, moreover, in exciting and original directions, without the slightest fear of experimentation. Many gardeners become more cautious as they grow older. Not Beverley McConnell.

PEAR TREE COTTAGE

———◆◦◆———

W HAT could sound more English than a property called Pear Tree Cottage? And it might be said (I said it) that this is a very English garden. But we are in Australia, I must explain.

My first visit to Australia, confined to Victoria, was as a speaker at the Australian Garden Design Conference held in Melbourne in October 1989. I enjoyed myself enormously and longed for the opportunity to return (without having to pay for the journey!). Among the friends I made was Michael McCoy, who was a conference delegate. He wanted the opportunity to come to England (I suppose he was aged twenty-five or twenty-six at the time) and managed it for the summer of 1991, spending quite a lot of time at Dixter and volunteer gardening for me for six weeks.

It was Michael who set the ball rolling for my return visit, which was backed by the British Council, the Australian Broadcasting Corporation and the Australian Gardens Scheme, then expanding to include several more states than the original Victorian starting point. I gave lectures, interviews and broadcasts and was allowed to have Michael as shepherd and chauffeur. There were 'free' days to see gardens and the bush and we saw a lot.

On my first visit I had become acquainted and subsequently friends with several people in West Victoria, notably with Roz Greenwood and Ann Dwyer, who run a most enterprising shop for old and new books in the provincial town of Hamilton. So we stayed with them this time at their home in Dunkeld, a few miles from Hamilton and close to a range of hills (if you're Scottish) or mountains (if you're not) called the Grampians. It was they who landed Michael and me, on the morning of 28 November (early summer for them), in Patricia Learmonth's garden, also in Dunkeld.

I wasn't expecting anything in particular, while noting in desultory fashion, as we walked in, a flock of honey-eaters squabbling around the blossom of a red bottle brush (callistemon). It wasn't long before I was properly awake. The garden quickly opened out and it was the best I'd seen during three

Roses, *Cistus × purpureus* and foxgloves make a foreground to the Grampians in the distance.

weeks in Australia. We had evidently struck the right moment and I heard none of the usual complaints or excuses to be expected of self-conscious garden owners, apart from that of excessive and exceptional rains. The garden is flat, the soil clay, and in spite of raising the level of some beds a little, quite a number of plants had died of waterlogging. I couldn't see the evidence. In high summer, drought becomes the problem and irrigation (company's water) is laid on, as it was in every garden I visited.

The house looked traditional; single-storeyed, red corrugated iron roofing, bull-nosed verandah supported by slender, cast-iron pillars. The strongest feature in the garden is a palm-like *Cordyline australis* standing architecturally at one corner of the house. Pat Learmonth planted it soon after her arrival, fifteen years before. It never stops shedding leaves, which have to be picked up every morning (all evergreens are like that), but I find these cordylines impressive and it was in full bloom at this time, the clusters of white blossom softening it delightfully. It is sweetly scented, too, but at close range, which is difficult to attain once tree-like proportions have been reached. A Virginia creeper, *Parthenocissus quinquefolia*, grows first up its trunk and then across to the house eaves, and colours a brilliant, yet kindly, red in autumn.

Best use is made of any protection or support the house will afford to plants, and the difference between their climate and ours is at once apparent by the wealth of blossom on pelargoniums, which survive the winters and attain a big spread. At one sunny corner of the house, for instance, the peppermint-scented *Pelargonium tomentosum*, with broad, softly furry leaves, had run up to the guttering and was smothered with tiny, pale mauve flowers, which could easily be dismissed as insignificant, but not when carried in such profusion. Besides, there was a yellow nasturtium peeping out from its skirts. And more nasturtiums running up the stiff legs of a 'Parkdirektor Riggers' rose, which was way above the roof line. This has single red flowers over a long season, if not allowed to run to seed.

At the other corner of this end of the house, a double cream white Noisette rose, 'Lamarque', was tumbling over the verandah's pillar and there was the Mexican daisy, *Erigeron karvinskianus*, at its feet. That had sown itself everywhere, just as in my own garden. The rose, which dates from 1830, is one of many climbers you'll see and admire in a climate like this or the Mediterranean, but which, you'll be chagrined to learn, is barely hardy enough to grow outside in our climate, unless it be in the mild south-west.

I should like to mention the very pleasing brickwork which forms curved paving around the end of the house, with the plants I have been describing on the inside of the curve. Pat designs gardens and is sensitive to materials as well as to layout. Bricks are again well used in a part of the garden which she

A bowl of sempervivums at the centre of brick paving with beds of colourful salad crops. Roses and white valerian (*Centranthus*) predominate behind.

wanted to remain rather open and spacious, where she has created a formally designed, circular feature. There is a low container in the centre, packed with sempervivum. This is surrounded by brickwork in concentric circles. Beds shaped to the sectors of a circle, but with truncated noses, are planted formally with colourful salad crops, the most noticeable of these having large, purplish leaves. Pat calls it serafin, but I think it must have some other name. Anyway, it is a pretty feature. Elsewhere, local sandstone from the Grampians has been used for steps and paving.

There is an acre of garden. It was a paddock fifteen years before, with two pear trees the only saveable contents. A row of twenty-six overbearing macrocarpa cypresses ran along the south boundary and were felled, their roots being left to rot. A backcloth rather than protection has been provided here and there by the exceedingly fast-growing *Eucalyptus bicostata*, which might well be treated as a bedding plant in Britain, as we do the nearly related *E. globulus*. Tasmanian blue gum is one of its popular names. It is not at all long-lived but does a job quickly and can be pollarded, if you have the energy.

The garden would be dead flat, had not Pat's neighbours, before she came, excavated a pond – ponds are called dams, in this part of the world – on the boundary, throwing the clay excavation on to their neighbour's land. This mound, in fact, proved to be an excellent opportunity to create a feature from which to get an overlook. In order to be able to grow plants on it, Pat imported 10 tons of soil. She now really needs to own the pond! Its planting would make an excitingly different feature. A path leads up and around the back of the mound. There used to be a eucalyptus at the back whose shade justified the description of 'woodland walk'. Unfortunately the eucalypt died or was blown down. Anyway, it has gone and the woodland with it. I find that my shade-loving plants will often do as well when they find themselves, through similar causes, fully exposed, but the Australian sun is a lot fiercer than ours. I even felt the desirability of a hat once in a while, which is never the case at home.

Pat Learmonth, while appreciating the value of viewpoints (there is a smashing one, between her own trees, of a Grampian peak), also takes note of the fact that a garden should not all be seen at once. It should lead you on, not with a series of set views, but so that you are constantly encouraged to stop and look around you in several directions at a series of changing tableaux. In this way, though not in its contents, it reminds me of Ruth Bancroft's Californian garden (see page 165 *et seq.*).

There is one enclosed area, the herb garden, which is entirely secluded from the rest, and this, funnily enough, was the only area in which I did not feel entirely comfortable. It may largely have been because the little-beds concept of herb gardens and the frequently weedy aspect of the ingredients make them extremely difficult to bring off, visually. That said, it did include charming features, particularly as you approached through an archway of 'Félicité et Perpétue' roses and looked towards an 'Albertine' rambler on the far side. Both were in pristine condition at that moment in the year. A bold grouping of angelica was also helpful.

Roses are a powerful theme in this garden. They do extraordinarily well, but these things don't just happen. Or only up to a point. Pat doesn't have to spray against mildew. To see the pink, incurving clusters of 'Raubritter' without it made this charming rambler well nigh unrecognizable. But she does have to cope with black spot. Her Hybrid Tea and Floribunda roses make large shrubs and are integrated with other plantings. 'Roses are too ugly by themselves,' was the reply to my comment. If only there were more gardeners to appreciate this point.

The soft and stronger orange shades of 'Apricot Nectar' and 'Woburn Abbey' were dominant in late November, and the latter consorted happily with pink 'Retro', having self-sown white valerian (*Centranthus ruber*) filling in all about them. Another splendid companion for such roses is *Lavandula dentata*, then in full bloom and weeks earlier than the *L. angustifolia* cultivars which have given us the hardier lavenders like 'Hidcote'. In most of England we have to treat *L. dentata* as a bedding plant and it is worth the trouble for its deckle-edged leaves, its long flowering season and its strong aroma. But, except perhaps in the south-west, we cannot expect to see it making those large, prosperous bushes which depend on winter survival. It is exactly the

Looking across *Tanacetum ptarmiciflorum* and rose 'Apricot Nectar' towards the barn on the garden's far side.

same story with *Tanacetum* (*Chrysanthemum*) *ptarmiciflorum*, here seen cheek by cheek with 'Apricot Nectar' roses. In England (especially in parks) we grow this as a grey foliage plant for summer bedding, say with pink *Begonia semperflorens*. The leaves are spoon-shaped and finest filigree. But give it its head, with a frost-free winter, and wow! – does it take off, making a bulky 4-foot shrub covered, in early summer, with puffs of white daisies.

Such roses, which are bright, though not garish (and I would describe white roses like 'Iceberg' and 'White Spray' as bright), do not give an easy time to the muted purplish tones of a Gallica like 'Cardinal de Richelieu'. Enthusiastic though the Old Rosarians are about this 1840 product, I shouldn't hesitate to give him a miss, myself.

It would be interesting to see this garden in February (our August) and what was blooming then. Obviously the Cardinal would be at his dimmest; no bloom on 'Félicité' or 'Albertine'; some on 'Albéric Barbier'; definitely second crops on the others and, no doubt, on the valerians, assuming that they are cut back immediately after their first blooming. No foxgloves, of course. White ones looked inspiring in front of creamy white 'Albéric Barbier'.

One of the nice things about this garden is the settled appearance it has gained thanks to a great many self-sowers creating a tapestry effect. I have mentioned valerian, foxgloves and Mexican daisies. The pale yellow spikes of

Rose 'Albéric Barbier' and white foxgloves.

Sisyrinchium striatum are plentiful; *Lychnis coronaria* (a lot of the white); opium poppies; love-in-a-mist; forget-me-nots; *Verbena bonariensis* (quite a serious weed of arable farming, in some areas); while dwarf gladioli such as 'The Bride', even if not actually self-sowing, multiply so abundantly from pups as to behave like do-it-themselves.

Pat loves a good plant, whether for its foliage or its flowers. A variegated coprosma, with broad white margins to a highly polished leaf, seemed to me to be performing the same function as *Euonymus* 'Silver Queen' in my own mixed border. *Salvia aurea* was interesting. Tolerant of very dry conditions, it is on the mound; shrubby, with rusty brownish yellow, hooded flowers. Another good labiate, which we see quite a bit in England, is *Phlomis italica*, a woolly, grey-leaved shrub with slender spikes of pinky mauve flowers borne in interrupted whorls. Why aren't I growing it?

Solanum rantonnetii, with a long succession of rotate purple nightshade flowers, looked excellent interleaved with an abelia having lime green foliage. We can grow the solanum on a bedding-out basis. The shrubby *Echium fastuosum* (hardy in the Isle of Wight, perhaps) carried its broad blue spikes of bugloss blossom in spring and was here well matched with the grey foliage of *Helichrysum petiolare*, though I have seen it even more dramatically paired, in another Victorian garden, with white arum lilies.

Agapanthus do too well, in these parts, though it seems unfair to denigrate them. In this climate, they have already started flowering in late spring and continue for several months. But their growth is somewhat boorish and Pat intends moving her large colony on to Council's land by the roadside, where

Golden-leaved abelia intertwined with the purple blossom of *Solanum rantonnetii*.

she has also recently created a bed for Australian natives.

There are not many of these in the garden proper. It isn't that they are deliberately shunned, simply that Pat uses whichever plants she fancies and which will grow for her, no matter where their origin. That, I reckon, is what makes this an English-style garden, if a style has to be assigned to it. Certainly it isn't French, nor Italian.

The English were the first to use plants for their own sake on any scale. They were overseas traders in a big way, which enabled them to bring in a huge assortment of species from foreign lands. Our climate was congenial to growing a wide range of plants, but too much should not be made of that, I think. The climate of a garden such as Pear Tree Cottage is also, with a little help, favourable for many plants, not a few of them far more easily grown there than in Britain, where we have to resort to greenhouse protection. There are gains and losses in most temperate gardening climates. If there is an English style, and I think we may claim there is, it is one that tends to embrace the opportunities afforded by soil and climate to grow many kinds of plants well and, one hopes (though this is not to be taken for granted), to present them flatteringly. Pat Learmonth is certainly in this tradition.

POSTSCRIPT

Pat and our mutual friends are emphatic that her garden is still a wealth of colour and interest in February, and from photographs sent me, I have to believe them (though I should have anyway). As suits that season, when hot weather makes you want to enjoy the garden (in the intervals between watering and dead-heading) at dusk, as it is cooling off, there are many grey-leaved and white-leaved plants preponderating. *Gaura lindheimeri*, its flowers hovering like insects, is a great favourite of mine, as are white cosmos, grown there with white and pink roses 'which looked fairly banal' until the cosmos joined them. White spider flower, *Cleome*, is another good 'un. Double white feverfew seeds itself all over and needs strenuous cutting back in between flushes.

The pale pink chalices of *Oenothera speciosa* (not quite hardy with me) are a joy though it is invasive. There are old-fashioned perennial asters (Michaelmas daisies, to us) in shades of maroon and mauve, and the long-lasting, lavender-coloured *Aster × frikartii*. This is interspersed with catmint in a rose bed. Red cannas below the sharp, scarlet pillar rose 'Altissimo' (so good for cutting), with the dwarf red Floribunda 'Marlena' at their feet, put body into the scene by day.

DALVUI

———◦◦———

SIZE AND SCALE make a great difference to a garden. Pat Learmonth's one acre at Pear Tree Cottage received the cottage garden treatment and responded admirably to it, although an acre, in England, would be considered vast by cottage standards. Dalvui, to which Michael and I drove on the afternoon of the same day, 28 November, is 20 acres. (Though it didn't seem as much, but then I have been told by my host that I haven't seen it all, being always in too much of a hurry, thinking about my next meal. Referring to my increase in circumference since our last meeting, he said I was 'putting on condition', a phrase used by cattle raisers, of whom he is one. With Ray Williams for a friend, what need of enemies?) Roses, here, would look totally inappropriate, apart, perhaps, from the sort that will hoist themselves up big trees.

I first visited this garden with members of the Garden Design Conference on 1 October 1989. We were given lunch and remained till 4.30. Beth Chatto was with me and we monopolized our host, much delaying the start back on a long return journey to Melbourne, but we were totally absorbed. I couldn't wait to return. This time it was just Michael and myself, and Raymond Williams, the owner, instead of being 'clothed in white samite, mystic, wonderful', as on the previous occasion, was in his working clothes. But he was the same person, not letting me get away with much.

Guilfoyle (William Robert) is a name to conjure with in the field of Australian landscape design at the turn of the century, and he laid out the gardens at Dalvui in 1898, four years before the building of this very typically Edwardian house was started. He had an excellent sense of scale. The garden stands well back from the house, allowing excellent views from the windows. The lawns are spacious enough to accommodate full-grown trees, as they now are, but not so vast as to make you feel lost on them. Some of his detail, like the rock garden, assembled with a peculiarly nasty volcanic rock, is hideous.

So now it is Raymond Williams's turn to leave his mark. He will have

Dalvui, West Victoria.

been imprinting it for ten years by the time this is published. His motto could be 'Learning to Live without Guilfoyle'. He does not despise his legacy, but neither does he worship the past because it is the past, like so many conservationists. Their reverential attitudes are largely an admission of sterility in their own thinking. It is easier to copy than to create. For Ray, creativity is in his fingertips. He loves gardening and does it all, in addition to having to give his attention to the farm on average two hours a day, with the help of one full-time gardener.

He has the rare and, in this context, necessary capacity for thinking big; that is, for being able to plant on a large scale so that you can admire from a distance. That does not have to preclude the study of detail near to, on occasion. But intimacy is not appropriate all the time. This is a garden in which you can breathe.

The house is dramatically approached along a broad drive which describes a curve, with trees on either side. Unfortunately a number of these were uprooted in a storm, between my visits. One has to be phlegmatic about such visitations. Birches (some of the victims were birches) are not long-lived (only fifty years on my soil), but neither do they take long to make an impression after planting.

An interesting feature set in the lawn on your left as you come close to the house is a semi-circular *patte d'oie* of flower-beds, with discreet brick coping to protect their outlines. There are six of them, separated by strips of grass, and they are wedge-shaped, forming the sectors of a semi-circle. Originally, they were presumably bedded out. Ray hates bedding, so what would now be appropriate? At my first visit, they contained hummocks of *Erica carnea* in bloom, the large gaps between representing callunas which had died. Ray expressed himself entirely satisfied with the heather idea.

This time the same heathers, higher now, were still there and we were told that they would be coming out, but not what the proposed replacement would be and we didn't discuss the subject, but I shall be interested to see what is decided on. I like a feature of that kind and wouldn't mind taking quite a bit of trouble over it. After all, it's something you are intimately aware of every time you go in and out of the house.

One of the big groupings that you can see from here, across a lawn, is of the long, dense vertical spires, bright crocus yellow and vivid in the landscape, of *Wachendorfia thyrsiflora*. The plant is 7 or 8 feet tall, prolific in the number of spikes produced, and the flowers are arranged, as in mulleins, in short

Giving scale: Lloyd with *Wachendorfia thyrsiflora*.

spikelets along the spike, so there are a great many of them. It can be grown outside in a climate like Cornwall's and I am inclined to have a go, as it is easily raised from seed and doesn't take long to reach flowering size (if it survives, that is). Of course there are always drawbacks about having the things you most desire. The tufts of iris-like leaves below the spikes are often pretty scarred with dead patches and there's not much to attract you out of the flowering season.

Near here is the New Garden – so called because it was made by Ray not so long ago. The New Theatre in London retained that name for the best part of a century, before it was changed to the Albery. New College, Oxford, has lasted a good deal longer and is now one of the oldest. Perhaps that is ripe for a change. The New Garden is formally divided into clipped box-edged beds, whose contents are informal and allow room for quite large shrubs and other plants. A mouth-watering group, for instance, of a purple-leaved eucomis. Another corner feature is the yucca-like *Doryanthes guilfoylei*.

I wouldn't have given space to the deutzia, which was in flower – what second-rate shrubs they are – but was greatly taken by *Escallonia organensis*, then covered in pink buds on wide panicles. It comes from valleys in the

Yucca-like *Doryanthes guilfoylei* in the New Garden. A mauve hebe in full bloom.

Organ mountains in Brazil, so it is a pity that we should actually be calling it *E. laevis*. Hardy against a warm wall in Cornwall but I don't know if anyone is growing it in Britain.

Elders grown for their foliage, like the white-margined *Sambucus nigra* 'Marginata', give their best display and largest leaves if pruned hard back each winter, but Ray actually cuts his to the ground, which I hadn't thought of but which makes this shrub a possibility where space is restricted.

The main part of the garden is on the other side of the drive and the dominant feature seen from the house, across a big lawn, is the cockscomb, *Erythrina crista-galli*. Pollarded hard back, each winter, to a wide-spreading framework of branches (so that each branch ends in a swollen lump), it has become a grotesquely magnetic attraction. Unfortunately I have been too early to see it flowering, when it is transformed into a mass of red pea flowers, borne in loose spikes. At that time (January–February), there is a haze of blue agapanthus beneath it and a jacaranda, not far off, continues the blue theme,

The grotesque winter framework of a pollarded cockscomb, *Erythrina crista-galli*, which will carry two crops of its red pea flowers in summer.

as much on the ground, with its fallen blossom, as on the tree itself. Under the erythrina, at the time of my visit, an extensive carpet of *Campanula poscharskyana* was flowering in a good, definite shade of blue.

There are some excellent plantings in the long, raised bed either side of the erythrina (itself on this mound); this used to be a rock garden and some rocks do still show through. Many, however, Ray has recently been able to get rid of while filling in an unloved swimming-pool, near by. Besides the agapanthus, big swathes, here, of white Japanese anemones, while *Verbascum bombyciferum* seeds around freely. Actually I think it is *V. phlomoides*, but the one I should really like him to have, here, is *V. olympicum*, for its nobly branching candelabra. The big leaves of a *Fatsia japonica* dominate one end of the mound, while a purple corylus is at the other – this needs frequent stooling for best foliage effect.

Around the back of this barrow-shaped mound, where there is a broad pathway running alongside it, grows a great colony, flowing among the rocks, of a glaucous-leaved echeveria, each rosette jostling its neighbours. Turn in the opposite direction and the view opens up. The tall, slender evergreen tree is a blackwood, noted for its fine timber but unexciting in flower, unlike most of the wattles. This is *Acacia melanoxylon*. In front is a fine cluster of *Cordyline australis* and just to the right of that a close relation of the pittosporums, *Hymenosporum flavum*. This was covered with its terminal clusters of waxy yellow blossom, strongly perfumed at night.

The path soon takes you into double herbaceous borders, which in January have the mauve pouffs of *Thalictrum aquilegiifolium* spilling out of them as they self-sow freely. *Aruncus dioicus* makes bold clumps and *Macleaya macrocarpa* stands out against the hedging. Ray rates highly a campanula that I don't know. Easily raised from seed, no one is offering seed. It is *Campanula primulaefolia*, whose leaves form a primrose-like basal rosette in the dormant season. It makes a handsome 3-foot panicle of sizeable, rather open, upward-looking bells of a decent blue colouring. The leaves are furry.

Ray pays great attention to plants with big leaves, as they stand out in a spacious setting and foliage lasts so well. For instance, he goes for the aroid *Alocasia macrorrhiza*, known as elephant's ears. He has planted a fig, *Ficus macrophylla*, whose evergreen leaves are up to 10 inches long. Known as Australian banyan, it is a tree which, like the true banyan of India, makes aerial roots which grow down to ground level and there take root. It will be gathered that frost is not a problem. He loves wigandias, which have mauve flowers and huge, hairy leaves. They can be raised from seed and treated as annuals for subtropical bedding, in Britain. Where is the seed?

Helichrysum petiolare 'Limelight' is good for lighting up a shady place near

to trees and doesn't take readily to scorching sunlight, anyway. In these countries, this species is perfectly hardy and makes a large bush, best cut back hard annually. At Dalvui it goes with blue agapanthus and a group behind it of the umbrella-leaved *Cyperus alternifolius*, which we grow as a house plant, though it takes well to being planted out in summer and can be treated as an aquatic, in shallow water. Ray declares his is *C. longus*, which is a British native that I grow in my pond year round, but he's wrong (I won't say 'I'm sure he's wrong' because that makes it sound as though I'm not sure).

Having gone round the garden, you have gone round the house. Close to the projecting porch is a tall urn on a pedestal containing more helichrysum, which cascades down to the ground (though without concealing the urn), and with it a climbing plant, the golden chalice vine, *Solandra nitida*, here treated as a cascader, with long tubular flowers that open wide at the mouth; gold, with chocolate brown markings.

From the sublime to the bathetic, what should we find on a prominent corner, here, but our old friend the ever-popular golden juniper, *Juniperus × media* 'Pfitzeriana Aurea', which has been the ruin of many a garden, both large and small. On account of its wide elbows, which it spreads over

Doryanthes guilfoylei here strengthens a bank of *Helichrysum petiolare*.

lawns or other plants, it has to be cut back at the margins and looks horrible ever after. But I should never dismiss a plant out of hand and here it is both strong and gracious, reaching out over the hard-core driveway. How long it can be allowed to do this before the scissors have to be taken to it, I do not know, nor how Ray will or can prevent it from looking the usual fright thereafter. It will be interesting. He could always move the drive – and the porch, come to that.

If there are areas in this large garden which one feels are still weak, you may be sure that Raymond Williams thinks so too, and will get around to tackling them in the coming years. What he has already achieved is inestimable. Both Michael and I were hugely stimulated.